In the CLUTCH
of CIRCUMSTANCE

In the CLUTCH
of CIRCUMSTANCE

Reminiscences of members of the Canadian
National Prisoners of War Association

Edited by

TONY STRACHAN

CAPPIS PRESS

**VICTORIA, BRITISH COLUMBIA
CANADA**

ISBN 0-919763-10-3
1. World War, 1939-1945 – Prisoners and prisons, German.   2. World War, 1939-1945 – Prisoners and prisons, Japanese.   3. World War, 1914-1918 – Prisoners and prisons, German.   4. World War, 1939-1945 – Personal narratives, Canadian.   5. World War, 1914-1918 – Personal narratives, Canadian. I. Strachan, Tony.
D805.A2152 1985   940.54'72   C85-091244-X

Published by:

CAPPIS PRESS, PUBLISHERS
1119 Oscar Street
Victoria, British Columbia
Canada
V8V 1X3

*"In the fell clutch of circumstance
I have not winced nor cried aloud."*

W. E. Henley: *Echoes (Invictus)*

*"Had I died, what would the world have gained,
Or lost?
For better men than I have gone and in their going
Immeasurably progressed the future.
But had I been chosen, would that passing
Have left its filial endowment to posterity?
For here, in escrow as it were, I realise
The Earth needs me not to move,
Yet I depend upon my fellow men —
So, in retrospect, I am myself in debt
To society for sustenation —
And owe the world a living."*

Hugh Mooney: *In Retrospect to an Escape from Death*

To the memory of

TED MUSGROVE

President of the National Prisoners of War Association,
1973-1981

ACKNOWLEDGEMENTS

Special mention should be made of the late Norman Rubenstein, former President of the B.C. Chapter, National Prisoner of War Association, who initiated the project and was responsible for taping many of the interviews contained in this book.

Special mention should be made of the late Norman Rubenstein, former President of the B.C. Chapter, National Prisoner of War Association, who initiated the project and was responsible for taping many of the interviews contained in this book.

Thanks also to Earl Taylor who so ably picked up the reins after Mr. Rubenstein passed away.

The directors of this project wish to express our sincere appreciation of the steady support and professional judgement of our publisher, Ed Gould of Cappis Press.

Donor List

New Horizons Program, Health and Welfare Canada
Fiberglass Canada, Toronto, Ontario
Rothmans of Pall Mall Canada, Don Mills, Ontario
U.A.P. Inc., Montreal, Quebec

CONTENTS

Introduction

Introduction

During the Second World War the majority of Canadians who were prisoners of the Japanese were captured at Hong Kong in 1941. The fact that they were captured in one place was a contributing factor in enabling them later to form a cohesive organization whose aim was to fight for compensation for the treatment they had received during their incarceration. (Even so, it took many years before they received tangible acknowledgement of their plight.)

Those who were prisoners of the Germans, on the other hand, were captured in many different places and at many different times. The largest group were those who fought at Dieppe; the rest were airforce, navy and army personnel who arrived at their captivity through a variety of routes and who remained prisoners from a few weeks to more than five years.

After the war the bigger groups formed prisoner-of-war associations. Each petitioned the government separately and fruitlessly for many years until some Members of Parliament voiced the opinion that unless the petitioners presented a united front they stood little chance of receiving a serious hearing from Parliament.

At the Dieppe prisoner-of-war convention held in Winnipeg in 1970 some of the more enlightened members decided that this opinion should be taken seriously. The mandate to form a National Prisoners of War Association was given to Ted Musgrove, Doug Dunn, Ed Duplessis, Bill Johnson, Howard Large, Jack Leopold, Tom McDermott and Ward Roach.

The first convention of the newly-formed association followed rapidly, in 1971, at Windsor where Doug Dunn was elected president. He was succeeded in 1973 by Ted Musgrove who remained in office for eight years until 1981 when he decided not to stand for re-election. Bob Large then took over.

In the following years the Association chalked up an impressive list of accomplishments. The membership expanded to well over a thousand, with eleven chapters reaching from Halifax to Victoria. In 1985 it included veterans from several wars, most theatres of operation, all branches of the armed forces and both sexes. Also included are Allied ex-prisoners who later came to this country and became Canadian citizens.

The organization is thus truly representative and, as such, has been able to present forceful arguments when dealing with government. Briefs presented to the Standing Committee on Veterans' Affairs, in conjunction with other groups, proved of inestimable value in attaining projected goals. In 1973 a *Study on Canadians who were Prisoners of War in Europe during World War II*, by J. Douglas Hermann, M.D., F.R.C.S. (C), F.A.C.S. was presented to the Minister of Veterans' Affairs. In April 1976 compensation was awarded to prisoners-of-war of the Germans during World War II followed, in 1978, by a similar award to prisoners from World War I. In October 1980 widows whose husbands had been receiving less than 48 percent pension were at long last given a proportionate allowance of the widow's pension.

Although the Canadian nation has been more generous in its treatment of its citizens who suffered captivity than other Allied powers, much remains to be accomplished in the area of both prisoners-of-war compensation and the widow's pension. Although the passage of years inevitably brings a diminishing of the number of survivors, the remainder continue to struggle for what they believe is their just recognition.

The National Prisoners of War Association is thus an active, if not activist organization. It is evident that the exchange of reminiscences in legion halls is by no means its primary function.

Those reminiscences, however, based on factual experience, remain none the less valid. It is the purpose of this book to place them on record, in permanent form, and before it is too late, in the belief that this nation's history would be the poorer if they were lost.

Dorothy Musgrove
Tony Strachan
Vancouver, August, 1985

1

My Six Years Of War

Robert V. Waddy

On September 3rd, 1939, I was eighteen years old. England had just declared war on Germany and I decided, as my father had in the First World War, to join one of the services.

So I joined the Canadian Army, 15th Coast Regiment, Vancouver, and went to York Island for training.

There we manned 4.7 guns. I remained for ten months, then transferred to the 3rd Light Ack-Ack and later proceeded to Halifax for an overseas posting.

I arrived in England in March, 1941. Our unit became Mobile Ack-Ack along the south coast of England until January, 1942. From then until May we were trained as commandos.

We all knew that something big was coming as there had been much speculation regarding a "second front." Suddenly all leave was cancelled and we were on our way to Portsmouth, and Dieppe. (We now know, many years later, that the Germans knew we were coming.) August 19th, 1942 is a day in my life I have tried many times to forget, but memories of the awful slaughter keep return-

ing. I consider myself extremely fortunate to have survived, as so many of my comrades were lost in those terrible
hours of battle.

At eight a.m. on the same day, after having survived,
and climbed those horrendous cliffs, I lay in a wooded area
of Dieppe and was forced to surrender myself to the Germans. I knew that I was too far inland to return to England.

We were rapidly transported by box-cars away from
Dieppe, as the Germans anticipated another attack. I was
now a prisoner-of-war.

We continued to travel by box-car to a prison camp
in France, that the Germans said had been built for them
by the French. We journeyed through France, part of
Holland, Belgium and Germany, finally arriving at Stalag
VIIIB, Lamsdorf. It had taken sixteen miserable days in box-
cars, each containing forty men, to reach our destination.
At VIIIB we were put in with East Indians and Lascars. We
were told that as we fought like "guerrillas", so we would
be treated the same as they treated "coloured" prisoners.

On October 6th, 1942 we were aroused at 0400 hours,
put on parade and informed that we were going to be tied
up, as Germans at Dieppe had been found washed up on
the beach "with their hands tied behind their backs." So
started a long period of being tied. It lasted a total of thirteen months. We were also deprived of our precious Red
Cross parcels.

I was fortunate, in that in December I was advised that
I was being transferred to a "Luft" or airmen's prison camp
as I was Ack-Ack, or "Flak" as the Germans called us.

There were three of us in the Ack-Ack at VIIIB, so off
we went to Dulag Luft I on the Rhine near Frankfurt. After
two weeks of interrogation we were sent by train to Stalag
Luft I, Barth, Pomerania. I was there until October, 1943,
then with the greater part of the camp was transported to
Stalag Luft VI, in East Prussia.

While enroute eight from my box-car, including myself,
cut our way through the barbed-wire window and escaped

Carrying in the morning "coffee" in winter was not the easiest chore.

from the train. After only six days of freedom we were picked up at Pasewalk, shipped back to Stalag Luft I, court-martialled by the "goons" and given one month in cells, after which we were sent by passenger train under escort, handcuffed, back to Stalag Luft VI, arriving approximately seven weeks after the original party. We were again court-martialled for being AWOL, and allotted another twenty-eight days in solitary, finally getting into the *lager* on January 8th, 1944.

I stayed in the *lager* until July 1944, then was evacuated by boat from Memel to Schweinemunde, as the Russians were advancing. We docked on the morning of July 20th, the same day that the dissidents tried to assassinate the Fuhrer. We were manacled together, barefooted, and raced four miles up to our new camp, Luft IV, with dogs biting and tearing at us and the Germans bayoneting us. We had many badly bitten and bruised POW's when we arrived at Luft IV.

After two months of being told that if Germany lost the

war we would all be shot I decided, with two others, to escape again, hoping this time to meet up with the Allies.

On September 20th, while on a fuel fatigue, collecting branches in the woods, we took off. We managed to avoid capture for five days but were eventually recognized by young German schoolboys, recaptured and sent to Berlin for interrogation; then we were transported to Stalag 344, the old Stalag VIIIB.

In early January, 1945 the Russians advanced and the whole camp was marched out through Czechoslovakia. We were constantly strafed by our own aircraft, as they had no way of knowing that we were POWs; consequently many were lost on this move. Finally we arrived, haggard and half-starved, at a large camp outside Munich. Thank God, after only two days we were liberated by General Patton's Third Army. It took approximately one week to sort out all the nationalities; then I was flown to Brussels and thence to England.

I arrived home in Canada on October 31, 1945. My six years of war had ended.

2

Hitler's Interpreter

Antoine Masson

Five days after the Dieppe raid nearly three thousand of us, mostly Canadians, were crowded into a German prisoner-of-war camp.

To the Germans we were just so many beaten, defeated officers and men for whom the war was over. The thing that bothered them was that they couldn't understand why the raid had taken place. They knew the force we used was not big enough to have attempted to form a permanent bridgehead, yet whoever heard of a ten-thousand man Commando raid? It is the unexpected that upsets Nazi military minds and Dieppe left them very upset.

I was a lieutenant in the Fusiliers de Mont Royal and we had been held as floating reserves. We were the last men to land and, while we fought well and served our purpose as a rearguard, many of us who survived were taken prisoners.

After a hasty grilling by Nazi intelligence officers on the spot we were moved to a large camp in the district which at one time had been a French military training camp. Conditions there were pretty bad. We had not been expected and scant preparations had been made for our arrival. Two small buildings were set aside for officers, and one hundred and twenty-seven of us were jammed into them.

The men suffered most during our twelve days' stay in the camp. Their quarters were cramped and the food was poor.

I had picked up some shrapnel in my right knee during the raid and most of my first day I spent in the camp hospital having it extracted. The German doctors were efficient, but the bedside manner was lacking. Since my wounds were minor next day I was able to hobble around our quarters.

Moving through hospital while I was there were broadcasters from Radio Vichy. They were carrying microphones from bed to bed trying to get men to give them stories. I learned later how Nazi trickery was employed by these quiz men.

Each broadcaster was accompanied by a Nazi officer. Every soldier knows that if taken prisoner and questioned he is expected to give his number and name. Our men did just this. The interviewer or the German officer would ask: "What is your number and name?" Men would answer, and the interviewer would follow up with "What do you think of Dieppe?" A French-Canadian soldier when asked what he thought of the raid surprised his interviewer by replying, "It was just fine. It just proved that we can beat the Germans any time." He managed to add something about what poor soldiers the Nazis were in man-to-man fighting. When the astonished interviewer came to his senses and cut the contact it was too late.

On returning to camp after being released from hospital, I found that Nazi intelligence officers were still calling our officers out for questioning.

High German army, navy and air force officials had flown from Berlin to check with their intelligence officers and to try their own hand at questioning us.

Late in the morning of my fifth day in camp, I was limping back to our quarters after having washed under one of the outside taps. I was carrying a towel over my shoulder and remember I had my own razor blade in my right hand. I was afraid of losing the blade as it looked as if it would have to do for a long time.

Near our quarters, I was hailed by a jovial grey-haired man in civilian clothes. He spoke perfect French and asked if he could chat with me for a few minutes.

There was something vaguely familiar about his face and I thought he must be pretty important in the Nazi scheme of things, as I had noticed a high ranking German naval officer saluting him.

I said that if he wanted to talk about the "show", as we termed the Dieppe business, he was barking up the wrong tree, but if he wanted to talk about the way we grow potatoes in Quebec, it would be a pleasure.

With a broad grin he said he would just like to have a man-to-man chat about Canada, as he had been on a moose-hunting trip there some years ago and loved the country.

He suggested that we walk over to a bench just outside an electrified wire fence surrounding the camp.

We went through the gate, and guards snapped to attention when they saw the man who was accompanying me. We went five or six feet outside to the bench and sat down.

I asked who he was, and he produced his wallet, plucked out an official German identification card and said: "I am Dr. Paul Schmidt." His card confirmed this. The pictures that had been shadowed in my mind came into focus.

I remembered Munich and Chamberlain's efforts to stave off war, and the pictures which had been published when the "Peace in our Time" agreement was signed.

I again saw photos of a stern Hitler, a grim faced Chamberlain and Henderson, and a grey-haired cheery man leaning over the Fuhrer's shoulder.

I also remembered pictures published after France collapsed, showing Hitler and some of his leaders at Compiegne. With Hitler was the same smiling civilian. That man was my companion. I handed back his card and said, "I remember you now from photographs published after Munich."

"I was, and still am, Hitler's personal interpreter, though other duties have been placed on me." Schmidt admitted.

I remembered other things I had read about Schmidt, his wide command of languages, his ability as a writer. I told him this, and added it was a shame to find such a man mixed up with a gang of cutthroats who were running Germany.

"We are supposed to talk about Canada," Schmidt grinned. He described in more detail his trip to Canada and his experience there. He said he was very attracted to my country.

I couldn't resist suggesting that perhaps what attracted him was all our vital living space.

Schmidt said: "Canada is a marvellous country. It has everything, but nobody has helped you to develop it. The British have left you alone in your wilderness."

I told him that most Canadians were pleased with the way our country had been run, and it was the desire to protect our way of living that had brought myself and many others to Dieppe.

I went on to tell him a few things I did not believe German travel books would have told of Canada. I said our country was a young country, but that a great future awaited it. There were English and French Canadians, and Italian and German Canadians, and a great number of other new Canadians living happily together.

I went on to tell him of people wanting to be governed by their own representatives, and that, while a country might develop more slowly under the democratic system, it was more firmly built. I said that no one man, even if he were a genius, could provide suitable government for a nation.

I asked if it were true that all important decisions in Germany were made by Hitler, and Hitler alone. Schmidt said, "Yes, that is true . Hitler is a genius." I said, "Well, as far as we are concerned he is an evil genius."

The smile left Schmidt's face. He looked at me solemnly and said: "Hitler is wonderful. I have been near the Fuhrer often when he is planning campaigns. I have seen him pore over maps, moving division after division from one front or from one sector to another. He is responsible for all we do. He, and he alone, is the brain of our organization. He is more than a man."

While Schmidt spoke of Hitler he was a changed man. He used his hands for emphasis and his eyes assumed an almost vacant expression of hero worship. I couldn't resist asking if it did not make him shiver when he realised the immense power Hitler possessed.

"When you see him moving men, don't you ever think of the people whose lives are dependent on those men — of their wives, their children, their mothers?" I asked.

"Does it never strike you," I added, "that Hitler is stopping the natural development of generations, and that he is applying their services to purely destructive purposes? Does Hitler not fear the wrath of all nations that are gathered against him, and does he not fear for the future of his own people?"

"You don't look deep enough," Schmidt said. "Much more is going on than meets the eye. The fruits of Hitler's work will change the course of the world for young fellows like you. Your generation and following ones will come to acknowledge the good work our Hitler is doing in introducing a new purpose in life for everyone."

It is not often that one gets the chance to talk to a Nazi of Schmidt's standing, and I decided to go all out in asking questions: "Don't you realize that, with America in the war and the growing might of all the Allies, you are going to be defeated?"

Schmidt looked at me steadily and replied: "If that happens we will continue fighting only so that we might obtain an honourable peace."

I got off the bench and stood beside him. I told him that I had enjoyed our conversation, as it had made me realize more deeply than ever before, just what we were fighting for, and that I only wished it was possible for me to answer his Nazi theories publicly so that the people of the world could choose between us.

I told him I was going to try to escape, and, if successful, I hoped the authorities would allow me to make our interview public.

Schmidt grinned. "Those are ambitious plans," he said, "but don't try to escape. I know it is your duty to do so, but you could never get away, and after this war is over we will be able to use young men like you for the reconstruction of the world."

I smiled back and said that I had my own plans for helping in the reconstruction of the world, but they followed democratic lines and that was why I had been fighting and why I hoped to get free to fight again.

He held out his hand and we shook hands. "I don't agree on many things, but I like the way you spoke up," Schmidt said.

We walked back to camp. Schmidt left me at the gate. Another officer had noticed me with Schmidt. I told him of our conversation and asked his permission to attempt to escape as the opportunity presented itself.

He patted me on the shoulder and said: "Go to it Masson and good luck, and when you get back to England, apart from telling them of Schmidt, get them to send me one hundred and twenty-six service uniforms as it looks as if some of us will be here a long time and we need new uniforms already."

Captain "Bud" Brown had also seen me with Schmidt.

I told him of our conversation.

A few days later we were moved to another prisoner-of-war camp and soon after Brown and I escaped.

We didn't get directly back to England, since we were picked up by the Vichy authorities. I escaped from them but almost fell into a trap set by the Gestapo. I finally arrived in Britain.

My proudest moment was when the King pinned the Military Cross on my tunic, but I was also happy and proud when I dropped into the army stores department and gave the officers order for one hundred and twenty-six complete service dresses.

EDITOR'S NOTE: A few years later, after the defeat of Germany, Dr. Schmidt had somewhat changed his opinion of his former Fuhrer. In an interview with the *London Evening Standard* he described him as "an amateur with considerable gifts. He could grasp a situation easily. But his trouble was he thought he knew everything."

The *Standard* interviewer pointed out that this verdict was at variance with that given to Captain Masson in 1942. Did he now deny that he had paid this tribute?

"Not a bit. It was just to make the officer — a charming man — talk."

3

A Woman In Shanghai

Gwen Dopson

Up until 1939 when Hitler invaded Europe the Far East was a very pleasant place to live and work. The extent of one's social life depended entirely on what one wanted to get involved in. We led a very reasonable life but things changed a great deal after September 1939 — for the worse I'm sorry to say. The Japanese had been active against the Chinese since 1937 and were gradually taking over strategic places and, of course, with the withdrawal of our British Forces from the Far East civilians became more vulnerable.

Leslie and I had met in Hong Kong where I was living with my parents and after a trip home to England I returned to Shanghai at the end of 1938. We were married on the 31st December of that year. Our daughter was born two years later but in the meantime we had assumed the responsibility of Leslie's son John by a previous marriage.

About 1940 various companies started sending their women and children back to their home country (England, the United States, Canada or wherever). However, there were others who did not feel that this was necessary and Thomas Cook's was one of these, which is why employees

Leslie Dopson — in Haiphong Road Camp.

of that firm were still in Shanghai and other ports in China when hostilities broke out. When the Japanese moved in and took over Shanghai in 1941 offices were closed and contact with home countries was cut off except through the Swiss Consulate.

At this time an organization known as the International Residents' Association was organized. They were a great help and did all they possibly could to act as a kind of liaison between us and the Japanese. It was at this time that

we were issued identification cards and forced to wear arm-
bands bearing an initial for nationality and a number (mine
was B 699). It also became increasingly difficult to make
ends meet and we, like many others, were forced to sell
many of our possessions to raise money to feed ourselves
and the minimum of servants we could keep. We were
reduced from nine to two. All our wedding presents and
any other valuables were auctioned off and some things
we had to hand over to the Japanese, such as radios,
cameras and various items for which we received a piece
of paper covered with Japanese characters. To do this we
often had to stand in line for hours and sometimes had to
return the next day. Also when disposing of our valuables
we had to choose an appropriate time when we would not
be likely to run into the Japanese parading the city in groups.
In this our servants were a great help. (Here I should mention that in order to keep any servants, and it was necessary
to have some around the house, we had to guarantee that
we would supply them with enough rice for a month at
a time. As you can well imagine, this was not easy, but
with the help of Chinese friends and others we managed
somehow. Money had depreciated so much that it was part
of their pay to have the rice and this, of course, got harder
and harder to obtain).

During the period that the Japanese were getting
organized to intern us it got more and more difficult to get
about and to obtain food. The Japanese would inflict
curfews whenever they felt like it and cordoned off various
areas. This meant that if you were caught in a curfewed
area you had to stay in that area, no matter what time of
day or night it was, until the curfew was lifted. Families
would usually go about together so as to be together if
caught in a curfew and also in case anything further happened. In 1940 when we were in Tientsin relieving the office people there for annual vacation my stepson John and
I were caught in one of such curfews and were forceably
inoculated on the street. We were told what it was for and

it was not very sanitary.

It was about 2 a.m. November 6th, 1942 that Leslie and I were awakened by loud banging on the front door.

Gwen, Leslie and Vivien Dopson in happier days.

The intruders did not wait for the door to be opened but forced it. Then they came up the stairs and located our bedroom where they ordered Leslie to get dressed and indicated they were taking him with them. Under such circumstances one does not argue, so he got dressed and was allowed to take one small suitcase with some clothing and toilet articles with him. The Japanese then proceeded to seal most of the rooms in the house by putting stickers across the doors with the exception of the bathroom, kitchen, childrens' bedrooms and the main bedroom. They took Leslie away and I had no news of him for about ten days when I was told that I could send more clothing to him.

Sometime during that ten days the Japanese came back to the house and after a very lengthy search removed the stickers and I was allowed the use of the whole house again. We had a very extensive library and they seemed particularly interested in the books, in spite of the fact that they appeared not to understand English.

The British Consulate together with the Red Cross were instrumental in getting more clothing to Leslie and the other men who had been taken into the Political Prison Camp known as Haiphong Road Camp. There were a lot of looters about and word had spread that I was sending clothes to Leslie. The night I had packed a trunk for him the house was burgled and all the clothes were taken as well as other articles, including all my silverwear, items in the dining room and my fur coat. I managed to round up a few more things for Leslie but the best had been taken.

I tried to trace them through the Chinese Police but had very little cooperation. Thinking back, I am glad that I was as young as I was (twenty-five) and had the children to think of, otherwise I don't think I could have been equal to everything that happened. I did get one or two letters, or I should say messages from Leslie but, of course, they could not obtain any real news. We had to just carry on, not knowing when our turn would come. We were, at that time, allowed Red Cross messages to family at home, in my case England, and were lucky enough to get a short reply.

It seems that when there is a war going on everyone seems to be at a high pitch and adopts the attitude of "live for today". We therefore had a number of house parties but always took the children along with us because of the curfews which might result in our having to stay the night. This happened on one or two occasions and it is surprising how everyone pitched in and slept where they could.

In April 1943 we were ordered to be ready to go into camps. Because Vivien was then only two years old and John eleven I was to go to a camp which was situated closer to town. Apparently the reason for this was the hope that we would get better supplies for them. As our group was going to be composed mostly of women and children, we were allowed, after much haggling, to take some type of bedding with us. We were not informed how many things we could take or how they would be transported but I took a chance and upturned a bed-chesterfield and filled the inside with things that I felt I would need even though we did not then feel it would be for very long.

It was April 3rd that we were rounded up in trucks and taken to Weiheiwei Road Camp. When we arrived at the camp our luggage was screened. I feel I was very lucky to be able to keep what I had taken as it all came in very useful.

The camp was a series of old disused British Army huts but fortunately most of them were divided, after a fashion, into rooms and we were allotted our space. This accommodation was *not* in good condition and was badly rat-infested. One man in camp managed to make some traps and caught eleven rats in my room alone in one night. Rooms were very small but with some juggling we managed to get them reasonably comfortable. Shortly after we were installed one of the other camps down river was closed and the men, most of them merchant seamen who had been caught, were spread around the other camps. In our case it was a great help as they could do some of the heavier

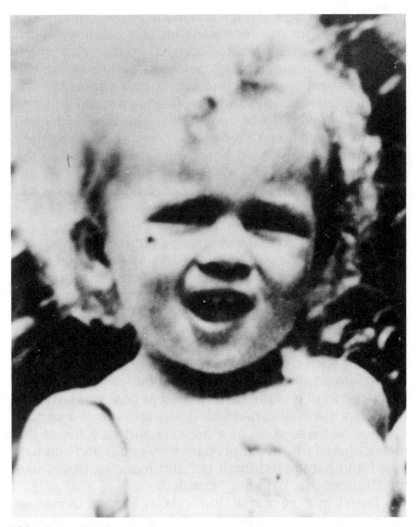

Vivien Dopson in prison camp.

chores.

One of these men who had been taken together with other businessmen was a friend of ours and he was invaluable to me, particularly with the children. He was also a handyman and he as well as other men stole slats from the sides of the huts at night and made rough furniture and some shelves for our rooms. As his profession was artist with one of the big firms in Shanghai he painted a mural on one wall for me. He also painted a picture of the surroundings and one depicting our various chores.

There were always rumours floating around and one was that we were to be repatriated. The Americans and Canadians went home after a very short stay in camp. Their Governments must have been more persuasive than the British!

Everyone, with very few exceptions, was put to work. For a time I helped with the Red Cross supplies. Then a girlfriend and I volunteered to help with the cooking, such as it was. Trying to make something out of what was sent in to us was not the easiest thing to do. We had a long shift and it was quite an experience to cook for four hundred and twenty people and to be complimented on the result. As time went on supplies became scarce and after several months we asked our liaison man to speak to the Japanese to see if we could have our supplies, no matter what, divided among each family or single person or couples, and we would look after our own meals. To our surprise they agreed and so all food was divided. As long as coal was sent into the camp it was also divided. It was found that a certain clay we had was good as a fire clay and so some of the men gathered up any empty cans they could find and flattened and hammered them out and made us stoves like the Chinese use, called a "chattie".

From a mixture of coal dust and clay some of us managed to make our own type of brickets to use on the stoves. The mixture was dried in the sun and was quite effective. We used these stoves from then until we were released.

In the summer we were allowed to cook outside and one evening when our meal was ready I called the children and Vivien came bouncing along and tripped and fell on the stove. She burned her bottom badly and had to lie on her tummy for a long time. When she was mobile, she almost had to learn to walk again. By rounding up as much as possible we found enough medication to treat her.

With our share of soya beans and the use of old Chinese grinders — two large pieces of granite with a hole in the top piece and a handle — we could produce a certain amount of milk for the children and later roasted the grounds which we used, kidding ourselves that it was coffee.

Red Cross parcels were not frequent and actually dwindled off for some considerable time until we were released. Clothing became a problem, especially during the winters which are always very cold in that part of China. Many of us pulled out old sweaters and re-knit them as best we could for the children. By pulling together and sharing our resources we were kept busy. Those who had contacts on the outside could arrange to have clothing and food sent in once a month. Unfortunately most of my contacts had also been interned, with the exception of one Russian friend who did what she could for as long as she could, but I did not have the resources for her to keep this up for very long. When she got sick I lost touch with her.

We were under very strict jurisdiction and had to be in our rooms with lights out by nine each evening. We were awakened by a bugle (proper military fashion) and had to be out and dressed ready for roll-call each day. The time varied considerably and sometimes this would also happen during the night. When there was a full moon, one of the Japanese officers who liked his saki took great pleasure in arousing us during the night and at times would take various people away for interrogation. Under the circumstances it was usually best to just do as you were told — if not, accept the consequences. Sometimes those taken away were badly treated and we would not see them for several days.

The lack of communication with loved ones was one of the hardest things to bear as well as no communication with friends and families in England. During our stay at

Weiheiwei Road as "guests" of the Japanese we were allowed to write Red Cross letters but were limited to twenty-
five words. At first these were allowed once a month but
as time went on they became fewer and fewer. One day
women who had husbands in Haiphong Road Camp were
told they were going to be allowed to visit their mates. I
was elated. But when the day came, my name was *not* on
the list. It is impossible to describe how I felt. Our aide-de-
camp, who had been a friend before camp days, was a great
help and did everything he could to find out why. After
a lot of discussions I learned that Leslie had been taken to
Ward Road Jail, which the Japanese were using as a
hospital, and told I would be allowed to visit him there.
It seemed an eternity to me but one day I was escorted to
the hospital and learned of Leslie's illness — cancer of the
throat. Apparently the Japanese doctors had been giving
him ultra-violet treatment which had caused the cancer to
grow. When I saw him his neck looked as though he had
an advanced case of mumps. It was a distressing visit but,
still, better to know what was going on. Soon after my visit
Leslie, through some Consular friends, managed to get permission from Tokyo to be moved to the Radium Institute,
which in those days was one of the most advanced hospitals
for cancer treatment. It was run by the nuns.

Leslie had an operation and cobalt treatments and remained in that hospital until the end of the war. It was
sometime after the Armistice that we managed to get
together to try to start our life over.

As for the children and myself, our life was much like
living in service quarters; fortunately most of us got along
well together. The children had school as we had a number
of teachers interned with us and for three months we actually had a dentist. But he was American and was soon
repatriated. While the dentist was with us I went to see him
about a wisdom tooth that was bothering me. He proceeded
to pull it out and also noticed some other little deformity
in my mouth so a few days later he attacked that but it was

not an easy job as the tooth had a screw root and after three hours and thirteen shots of novacaine I passed out, leaving the nerve exposed. I suffered with this for nearly a week and then it was arranged that I could visit a Swiss dentist on the outside, so I was escorted by the dentist and two Japanese guards. At the Swiss dentist's office one of the guards stuck by me all the time — maybe he thought I was carrying a message in my tooth! Today I am still not very partial to a visit to a dentist.

We had Chinese interned with us because they had been born in Hong Kong and were therefore British subjects. Two of them ran a flourishing black market. Most of us had managed to smuggle in some cash when we entered the camp, of course, some more than others, so if you had the money you could get some extras. As always, certain people keep together and there was a group of us without our husbands who would on occasion — especially during the first summer when we were still hopeful that we would be out "tomorrow" — celebrate a birthday. By using the black market, we would get a bottle of Vodka, which was distilled in Shanghai because of the large Russian population there. To cover up our actions we would have the Vodka in cups of tea and so could sit outside when we had a few free moments and celebrate the birthday. We were of course lucky not to be detected by the Japanese who were always walking around the camp. This didn't happen very often as our money soon ran out. In the beginning we were allowed comfort money but needless to say this was soon cut off and we had no other way of obtaining any. We did have one such celebration when we heard of the war in Europe being over.

Our own release seemed a long time after that and many of us stayed on in the camps as we had nowhere to go since most of our homes had been commandeered or looted by the Chinese.

Our first experience of imminent release was when the Americans came over in B-29's and tried to land large

drums of food. This almost caused another disaster as some
of the drums went through the roofs of the Chinese houses
around the camp; so the Americans went out further into
the country and then trucked the drums into us. These rations were divided among us and as we had been on such
low rations for such a long time some people ate too much
and became sick. Our rations for quite some time had been
whatever the Japanese could get and often resulted in just
"godown" sweepings that would include broken glass,
nails, coal and so on.

When we finally got out of camp we were housed in
empty apartments where we had to sleep on the floor.
Because of Leslie's condition we were some of the first to
leave Shanghai by British Hospital Ship. We were taken
to Hong Kong, which was quite a trip, lasting at least twice
as long as it should have due to mines floating in the sea.
Men and women were segregated — Leslie was at one end
of the ship, while I was down in the hold with the children.
We slept in hammocks and also ate our meals which we
had to get for ourselves from the galley located on the boat
deck. The second breakfast we had an unusual: tripe!

Again in Hong Kong we were housed in an empty
apartment but this time I did manage to scrounge a mattress for Leslie. After ten days we were flown by the RAF
to Sydney, Australia, with a stop off at Leyte in the
Phillipines where we grabbed a few hours sleep and then
were awakened at two a.m. and served breakfast before
continuing the rest of the flight. The breakfast being
American style, was in very large portions. We were still
not able to handle such large amounts of food. Before leaving Hong Kong I had found an old electric burner and boiled a dozen duck eggs separately in a cigarette tin. So with
those and some fruit and crackers we had been able to purchase we had something to supplement the K rations which
were given us on the plane.

After touching down at Fiji, Darwin and Conclurry we
arrived at Sydney, where it was 120 in the shade. There

we were housed in a Red Cross hostel until we could locate our own accommodation. Fortunately our man at Cook's soon found us a place at Manly. It was quite an experience for us and especially for the children to ride on a tram and share a taxi, and we were overwhelmed by the stores.

The Australian Government had offered us the visit to their country for Leslie to recuperate. We were there for six months before we sailed for England, a trip which took us via Suez, the Mediterranean and the Straits of Gibraltar to Southampton where my parents met us. We went to stay with them for a short time and then journeyed on to London to stay with Leslie's family.

From then on is another story. We came to Canada in April 1948, having had another year back in Hong Kong, where our son Brian was born in 1947. Leslie died in 1959 and Vivien in 1981.

Gwen and Leslie Dopson, marriage at the British Consulate in Shanghai, December 31st, 1938.

中華民國

中華民國年

指食左   指食右

十二月廿五日 日

Gwen Dopson and her identification.

4

Letters Of Internment

Muriel Garner

Gwen Dopson writes: Mrs. Fred (Muriel) Garner was the former wife of my husband. I had not met her until several months after we were married and she was by then Mrs. McBain, having remarried in Peking where she had met Mr. Garner who was at that time working in the Peking Consulate. She herself was Secretary to the British Ambassador to China. When the British diplomats were moved to Shanghai in 1939 Muriel and Fred came with them and it was at that time we became good friends. John, the son by her marriage to Leslie Dopson (my husband), had been sent to the boarding school at Chefoo but caused a lot of problems so Leslie and I decided it would be best for him to be with us as we could provide a home environment. For that reason John was with us at the time of hostilities and so came into internment camp with me and my daughter Vivien. Leslie had at that time already been taken to another camp (Haiphong Road Camp).

The following is distilled from four separate air-mail letters Muriel Garner wrote to me from London after the

*war, relating her wartime experiences in internment under
the Japanese.*

January 16th, 1946
My dear Gwen:

I can't ever begin to tell you how happy I am to have
had your letter. It is incredible to me that none of mine
have ever reached you. However, they may yet turn up!
In the meantime I will tell you our story.

After we had been in Sydney four months the F.O.
(Foreign Office) asked Fred if he would go to Chungking
for a few months owing to the Japs having held up the
release of our consuls and diplomats; they were terribly
short-handed. As we were absolutely frantic about you all
and were unable to get in touch with you (despite the
Australian Government's quite amazing helpfulness) we
decided to go, thinking we might be able to do something
from Chungking.

We duly set off on April 12th — having bought up
almost everything in sight in the way of drugs, soap,
medicines, creams, vitamins, oil capsules — goodness
knows what all for the kids — and five days out of Freeman-
tle we were awakened early one Sunday morning by the
yells of the Lascars as they called upon Allah to save them.
I grabbed my life-belt and rushed out into the corridor in
search of Fred (we weren't married then) only to find it was
a fake alarm. It appeared that a plane had flown over but
had failed to identify itself. We knew pretty well that it *must*
be an enemy plane, but with the invariable "it can't happen to us" attitude we did nothing about preparing an
emergency bag, but we *did* have a few beers and a huge
luncheon.

Having fed, we walked the deck until 2:30, when I felt
a strong urge to go down to the cabin and much against
Fred's will I persuaded him to come also. No sooner had
we settled down to read when we heard machine-gun fire

and a hail of bullets hit the ship. We grabbed our life jackets and rushed into the corridor where we flung ourselves onto the floor. Pretty soon we were being shelled heavily and the officers told us we were being attacked by a raider. We were under fire for one and three-quarter hours. The Captain and officers, assisted by several military officers who were passengers, put up a magnificent show, but finally it was obvious that the next salvo would sink us. The Captain gave the order to abandon ship. We were full of TNT but luckily also an enormous quantity of wool which saved our lives.

By this time there was no one to give any orders, so finally we pushed our way up to the smoke-room where Fred took charge and told everyone to take to the lifeboats. The firing ceased when the enemy saw our lifeboats being lowered and when we stepped out onto the deck the first sight to meet my eyes was a man sprawled out, his insides blown all over the deck, precisely in the place where we had been standing!

We finally got into the boats and as luck would have it my end went down and the other didn't, with the result that I was almost thrown into the sea. In the effort of saving myself my bag and all my possessions fell into the sea and were lost.

When we were finally launched there was no one to row — the Lascars had completely lost their heads: Fred and another man did our rowing for us. They were trying frantically to pull away from the side of the ship for fear of being sucked down with it. As we pulled away, an airplane flew low over us and we all felt sure we were going to be machine-gunned. We were not, however, and presently as we went along a huge ship came in sight and the order came along the line that we were all to make for it. Very soon we were able to distinguish the flag. To our intense relief we saw that it was not as we had feared: a Japanese raider. It was a German.

When we got alongside and saw hundreds of Germans

gangling over the side we were afraid, but immediately a rope ladder was flung over and we were ordered to climb aboard.

I never dreamed anything so awful could happen to me. I was hideously seasick and the fear of the sea, which is inherent in me, held me paralyzed for a few moments. I was, however, hauled onto the ladder by a huge German sailor, who had by this time gotten into the boat and I made my way up, swaying sickeningly until I reached the top. On arriving I was taken along endless narrow corridors and down and down into the bowels of the ship where I found several other women passengers. We were given hot cocoa to calm our nerves. There were thirty women and fifteen children. It was utterly terrifying battened down in those holds; I suffered agonies from claustrophobia for when the lights were switched off we couldn't see at all — we could only hear the sea beating against the sides of the ship as we tore through the water. We had been told by the Germans that regretfully if anything happened they would be unable to do anything to save us.

After two days of this misery we were allowed to go up on deck for half an hour's exercise and as we came back we passed the entrance to the men's hatch, whereupon I raised my voice in order to attract their attention and as a result Fred rushed to the opening and shouted "say you're Mrs. Garner, for God's sake" several times before the guards dragged him away. I then had to tell all those women what I intended to do and asked if they'd stick by me; they all readily agreed, so it was arranged, for Fred was afraid if we did *not* do this he might be released and I would be left behind.

After four days we were transferred to a "hell ship" called the *Reglusberg*. Our quarters were terrible; we lay on the floor with others in hammocks on top of us. We were in a hold and rats scrambled over us endlessly. It was a nightmare — we had to eat, sleep and do everything in the one cramped space. The Germans, however, were exceedingly good to us. On fine days we were allowed to spend a few hours each afternoon with the men. We were allowed to bring a few things from our cabins.

All my drug-store supplies had, however, been removed before I got back. We actually lost everything except the clothes we had with us. To make matters worse all my warm things were in the hold and as the hold stuff was regarded strictly as "the property of the Reich" I was not allowed to have even one warm coat.

Subsequently we were transferred to three other "hell ships" — the same trek from one to another in those terrifying rubber floats and the hideous climb up the rope ladders. Sometimes it was entirely too rough so they took us up in huge baskets. I don't know *which* was the more terrifying.

At the end of two months we intercepted a wireless signal and discovered to our dismay we were on our way to Japan where we were finally handed over on July 11th, 1942. We were sent up to a convent in Fukushima in the north where for twenty-two months we were absolutely lost to the world — no newspapers, no letters and, in fact, literally nothing — no medical attention and practically no food. For the first five months they tried deliberately to kill us by starving us but it is *so* hard to die if your time has not yet come, so we lived only two people died. Later we were given more food and after twenty-two months the Red Cross found us and we got one small parcel of food each.

We had no heat; the winter commences up north at the beginning of October and continues until the end of April. I received one card from my mother, in the March before the war ended — otherwise I had absolutely no news at all. Our men were mercilessly beaten up for so-called wrongdoing and we lived under a deep sense of fear. Everything was done to make our lives as great a hell as possible. I got so ill and so desperate I ended up by losing my head and attempting to kill a guard. I did not care what happened to me — in fact I hoped he would kill me, for

I had become so tired of the struggle to survive, and had long since given up all hope of living through to freedom. However, this shook them up a bit and the guards were told to lay off, which they did for a while.

It was only when the war news was especially bad that we had systematic reigns of hate which were awful. For the last nine months we were given only dry bread and hot water coloured with a few tea leaves which had rather the flavour of hot linoleum. We got a few Red Cross parcels; these were only a drop in the ocean, but they served to relieve the monotony. Although we were in the same building, we were not allowed to meet except on birthdays, wedding anniversaries, for fifteen minutes or sometimes half-an-hour under armed guard. Toward the end meetings were more frequent.

I think it was utterly disgraceful to separate *you* who were literally internees. I thought I should die when I heard the frightful news — knew that I was utterly cut off from you all for goodness knows how long. Every mouthful of food I ate choked me while I was in Sydney. I moved heaven and earth to get news of you and I suppose nothing got there? I'm dying to hear how John has developed. Is he more or less manageable now? He is a more reasonable age and should be a good companion. Where do you plan to stay in England.? Will you want hotel accommodation for a night or two? If so let me know and I will book immediately — hotel accommodation is like everything else — frightful! One is only permitted to stay five days! I hope to be able to meet you at the ship and if it is agreeable to you all will bring John back with me. I have only one small spare room otherwise I would happily have you all. This flat is a garret. One has to climb four flights of stairs to reach it and it's literally *full* of draughts! Everything, everywhere in London is pathetically shabby and dilapidated. I'm told it is a miracle we have found a flat at all. Four other people wanted it but as luck would have it the old boy gave me a break. I'm so delighted to have the spare room for John.

I want to see as much of you as possible while we are all here. I should *hate* to have to live here permanently, Gwen. There is no charm or dignity to life in London unless one is fabulously wealthy — so *much* is taken in income tax these days. Actually I detest running a flat, but Fred adores it so. I have a maid three half days a week. Fortunately there is a huge store quite near where one can buy everything — including booze. It's hell trying to make do on one's rations — especially when people in our rundown state need extra.

I long to be able to do some of the things we planned — unhappily conditions are not as we hoped and expected they would be, but we'll do our very best, never fear.

I'm so glad you are stocking up on clothes — the luxury tax is supposed to be coming off in April after which they will not be allowed to charge more than twenty guineas for a coat or suit! I've only bought one *lousy* suit and one teddy-bear coat. I wouldn't have looked at either of them before the war. In fact, I had the suit on the other morning cleaning the flat and the man from Harrods who came to check the inventory mistook me for the char!

Incidentally, our teeth simply rotted away in the camp and we've had to have fillings in almost all the back ones. I've been through hell with the drilling which I battle.

Does Leslie know that his brother Vivien died on January 1st of this year? I saw a notice in the paper which read to the effect that he died of a long & painful illness. I think it's better to know before arriving home, don't you? I prefer it that way myself. Of course I expect his father will write — but in case he doesn't — I have.

Will the time ever pass until I'm actually meeting you! Of course I won't recognise either Vivien or John. We are hoping to go on the Continent to our next post so that John can come over for his vacations. We will discuss everything when we meet — so difficult in letters.

Did the Japs take your jewellery? They took all ours about nine months before peace came to make airplanes.

Fred sends his best regards to you both. Take care of yourselves and eat all you can — drink oodles of milk. We only get half a pint between us per day here. I'm going to ask for a priority.

Has John grown out of those horrid little spasms he used to have in Shanghai? I do hope so. I shall anxiously await your further news.

My love to you and the children.

As ever, Muriel

Muriel Garner and Gwen Dopson in Shanghai in 1940.

5

Belgium Under The Occupation

Charles Despaey
from a taped interview

When the Germans attacked Belgium on May 10th, 1940, I was on leave from the Belgium army. We were all called back and we travelled to our lines where we were stationed. In the morning, the Stukas came over my home town, Ghent; the population was frightened, to say the least.

I was stationed on the Albert Canal, and nobody had any knowledge of what war would be like. One day the French and the English were driving their tanks towards the German border; the next day they turned back and they were almost flying.

The Germans were walking the one route and we were walking on the other — we knew the roads better than they. They followed the main line and we took the side roads and retreated over the Canal to Antwerp. Soldiers and civilians — the panic was something you have never seen in your life. The tunnel in Antwerp was full. We shot down a German plane. Needless to say, the retaliation was something fierce. They bombed the joint, and we retreated farther up to Bragen where, on May 28th, I was taken prisoner-of-war.

It was then that the King abdicated and gave the country to the Germans. The feeling for some was, well — it's over. Others tried to get away. We were marched back to Ghent, where I escaped to see my parents.

We were ordered to bring our military equipment, tunics and so forth, to the local police station. From there they marched us to a variety of places and we wound up in Holland. Then they shipped us on five Rhineboats to Emmerich, in Germany. It was "standing room only" — no water, no food — for five days. The ship was an old coal boat so we all looked like black people when we arrived. In Emmerich we were unloaded on a big field with a couple of taps, and it was almost impossible to clean yourself. Then we were transferred to a cattle train, eighty to a wagon, and pulled to Nuremburg where we got off. We were given water and some soup and, from there, we took another train where we were transported to Kremz where we stayed for six weeks.

After six weeks of malnutrition I was just a skeleton of my former self. We went to work in the mountains where we stayed until winter came. From there I was shipped to a little town in Austria where the song *O Tannenbaum* was composed.

The local population was a contrast to the Germans. Of course, you find bad ones among the good, but the Austrians were extremely nice to us. You have to remember that the Germans were standing over their heads. They were often afraid to give you something, although most of them were only too willing to do something for you, like giving you a piece of cloth to put your feet in or a piece of wood to make yourself a shoe with. Our clothes were worn out but you could get a needle and a piece of thread and sew it yourself at night, if you got a chance.

The first letter I got from my parents was in December so I knew that they were still alive and okay. They received a postcard from me which I still have — it was five months later that they received it. I also got one parcel from them with some chocolate and hankies, and so forth. We never received anything from the Red Cross but the French, next to us in a separate compound, received cherries in honey, among other things.

In the work camps the food was a shade better. It was still soup but there were potatoes in it, and once in a while we got a piece of meat. We were working on a radio station. At five o'clock we rose, and worked until seven or eight at night. At noon we had to walk back to the camp to eat, something like fish soup, but it was like the Connaught Hotel in comparison with the prison camp itself. At least you got something to fill your stomach with. But it was a tough job. You never stayed with two feet on the same level in the mountains. But the misery I've seen in the camps! There were Poles working down there. They had mules to transport equipment. On one occasion they were sent down with the guards to bring the mules up loaded with potatoes and bread. When the Germans weren't looking, they got needles, stuck them in the mules' eyes to blind them and ran off. So the Germans shot sixty Poles right there and then. It was cruel to the animals; especially since the escapees didn't really have any place to go. They were, in fact, asking for their own death sentence, as far as I'm concerned.

In February, 1941, the Flemish soldiers of the Belgian army were released, a thousand at a time. Only the hard core stayed in Germany. I was shipped back by train. They gave us bread and a chunk of cheese and we sat on the train for about four days until we landed in Holland. From there we went to Antwerp, where we were unloaded. I had family in Antwerp and they deloused me, taking off all my clothes and putting them in a kettle to boil. Then we were all called back to work as civilians in Germany. So I went underground into the White Brigade and ran reasonably free while keeping a low profile. Of course, the war went on.

My dad died in 1942, and I had two brothers and three sisters to support. I was a tile man and, in that trade, there was not much work, so we tried to work on farms, getting paid in potatoes or one thing or another that at least kept us alive.

The nightmares started when the British and American bombers came over. We were glad it happened but, of course, mistakes were made and sometimes they bombed the wrong places. There were six thousand houses demolished or partly demolished and about twelve hundred people killed, but that was part of the war and couldn't be helped.

When the 15th of August came around, it was my birthday. They were flying from the north of Africa over Germany on bombing missions and planes from England were flying to the north, so they were criss-crossing each other — I've never seen so many planes in my life. Thousands of them. They were buzzing and buzzing for hours.

In the Underground nobody talked to one another, nobody really knew what was going on; you were just told to do this or try to do that.

In Belgium, the telephone and the telegraph lines are built alongside the railroads. We would cut the telephone poles about half or three-quarter way through. When a storm came the wind would knock them over.

We also used to take nails out of the railroad tracks on a curve. When the train came up at high speed it would rip the rail right off. They were steam locomotives loaded with coal for Germany. That coal was ours in a jiffy. Everybody and his brother and sister was there with a bag. By the time the Germans got there the copper was gone, too. We just knocked it off with a sledgehammer. The copper was gone, the coal was gone — the train was as clean as a whistle, as if it had come back from a car-wash.

After D-Day. the Canadians and Poles took Ghent. The Germans were still on the other side of the Canal. They had blown up practically all the bridges in Ghent, and there are over one hundred of them. But the Poles crossed one that was still intact.

When VE-Day came the tanks' wheels were invisible because of the people hanging on to them. Sometimes a tank looked like a hearse full of flowers. In all the joy, it was difficult to believe that people had been killed.

After Antwerp was taken, food was distributed in no time flat. In 1945 we were eating rye bread while the English in 1950 were still on ration. When they got a couple of pounds they would come to Belgium to eat pastries because they couldn't get them in their own country. Meat was scarce in England while, just after the war was over, we had practically everything in Belgium. The reason was that Belgium had a nice pile of money stacked up in the United States. They wanted to repay us so they shipped us flour and butter and whatever was surplus to them.

But I found that living in Canada there was more food than anywhere in the world!

6

North Africa

Jack Garritty
from a taped interview

Malta had been besieged for a number of months. It was impossible to take aircraft carriers through the narrows, only twelve miles wide, which would have been the most direct route for the fleet which was to relieve the island. The plan was to approach the narrows, halt and then fly the Hurricanes and other aircraft off the carriers for the initial phase.

The enemy knew everything that was going on. The Spanish dock-workers where we left from were absolutely infested with spies, so there was no way we were going to fool anybody.

We took fourteen ships in the convoy, with a very large escort group. On the second day out the aircraft carrier, *Eagle,* was torpedoed. She went down in seven minutes. We got fifty fighters off the *Foreman* before she was hit and sank. We lost three or four more. The *Indomitable* was completely wiped out. There was a large loss of life.

Around midnight we were going through the Straits of Palermo when we were hit by three torpedoes and went down. We spent the following morning and all that night and the following morning in Calais floats, which hold about thirty people. There were about ten men inside the float, the wounded, with the rest with their hands on the side, swimming. We landed at eleven o'clock the following morning. We thought we were landing on neutral territory, but the Germans were waiting for us with machine guns alongside the shore. When we got on shore we found the airfields loaded with Messerschmidts and Stukas and the whole bit.

So we were taken prisoner. In the camp we had our Captain, the crew of an armed merchant cruiser, and the crews of the *Havoc* and *Legion,* and the remnants of six or seven different boats which had gone down. There was a motley crew of merchantmen, and two gentlemen from the Black Watch who had been at Dunkirk. They had travelled across France for thirteen months while their wives drew widows' pensions, and eventually reached Spain where they smuggled aboard a ship which turned them in.

The Captain of the *Legion* was one of the finest men I've ever met in my life. He was an older man who suffered in health very badly. We lost the doctor through polio.

The guards were Senegalese and petrified of us. If we made a move, they would fix bayonets. They had dumdum bullets, strictly against all the rules and regulations of war. Among other things, they pilfered our Red Cross parcels. Many times the parcels were full of sand. In fact, I don't remember many Red Cross parcels coming through. When we did get them, they had punctured every single can.

One night, twenty-seven of us tunnelled out. We were all back within twenty-four hours. It was the North African desert and there was nowhere to go. They just waited for us to return.

There was a price on our heads. The Arabs were offered five thousand francs for each of us alive, ten thousand dead. They preferred to have us dead.

It was just desert but it was level, and you could land

a plane anywhere. In fact, there was a little airstrip outside the camp. Our plan was to get out, steal a plane and fly to Spanish Morocco. We bribed a Senegalese guard who let one of our guys, a fighter pilot, get about half way through the wire and then they blasted him with dumdum bullets.

They did allow us outside to bury him in the desert. It was like something from the movie *Beau Geste*.

The Germans were going to transfer us to Italy, but all of a sudden North Africa was invaded. We woke up and everyone had vanished. Except for us, there was no one there at all. The gates were locked but the guards, all German staff, had gone. So we walked back to the station. An American plane flew in and dropped a few provisions. Somehow we got back to Algiers, the end of the line, where we commandeered a train which took us to the nearest Allied forces.

7

Norwegian Fiasco

Tony Strachan

The first German I saw was the one who captured me. I arrived in Norway on the evening of Thursday, April 18th, 1940, and was captured the following Monday afternoon. I was liberated on April 29th, 1945. Thus I had four days of active warfare, followed by five years of captivity. I was among the first half dozen British army officers to be taken in World War II. At the time of capture I was nineteen.

The background to these epic events is what was then called the "Phony War." At that time Germany was dependent on Scandinavia for much of its iron ore, as it had been before 1939. Allied dominance of the seas had placed this supply in jeopardy. Hitler was afraid the British Navy would mine the Baltic. The only route for the ore to reach Germany was through the Leads, the myriad islands dotting the Norwegian coastline. The Fuhrer was determined to secure it.

The Allies were equally determined to secure it.

The race was on.

For this important campaign in mountainous central Norway the British War Office in its wisdom selected a battalion and a half of the Territorial Army; amateur soldiers from two Midlands counties where no hill rises more than two hundred feet. Much of the previous winter, a particularly severe one by English standards and ideal for training in snow, had been spent by these troops attending anti-gas lectures indoors.

This force of six hundred men, eventually to be pitted against 120,000 German professionals, "lacked aircraft, anti-aircraft guns, anti-tank guns, tanks, transport, training," according to Winston Churchill in *The Gathering Storm*. They were plunged into a terrain "covered with snow the depths of which none had ever seen, felt or imagined. There were neither snow shoes or skis — still less skiers."

There was also no commander-in-chief. The first to be appointed had a fit on the Duke of York steps in London, and was carted off to hospital. The second had his aircraft shot down on his way to his command. By the time the third was appointed, the campaign was over. So he never got to Norway either.

The campaign was perhaps best summarized in a recently published history of 1940: "page 68, British forces land in Norway; page 69, British leave Norway."

During the first winter of the war, our troops were told they would be going to Finland, and were issued with fur-lined boots. Then they were told they were going to India. The boots were withdrawn, and the men were issued with tropical kit. When finally, on April 6th, 1940, they left their concentration area in County Durham, they were not told anything at all. So they clutched what equipment they had, and entrained in the dark. Such are the vagaries of troop trains that they did not arrive in Edinburgh, en route to the port of Rosyth, until April 9th, taking three days to cover a distance shorter than that from Vancouver to Kamloops.

As the train steamed through Edinburgh early that Sunday Morning, the bleary-eyed troops were greeted by newspaper posters announcing: "Hitler invades Norway." The force was put in camp in Dunfermline while the War

Office tried to decide what to do with it.

Meanwhile, the British propaganda machine went into action. "Look at the filthy Germans," it screamed. "They have invaded a neutral country."

Unfortunately, when later we were captured, all our documents were captured with us, and they proved that we had intended to occupy Norway first. So the Germans were able to proclaim: "Look at the filthy British. They tried to invade a neutral country. We only went there to protect the inhabitants from aggression."

Meanwhile, a week after our arrival in Dunfermline, the War Office made up what mind it possessed. The troops were marched to Rosyth, there to embark on the cruise liner, *Orion*. The ship was still being run on peacetime lines. Every morning, white-coated stewards promenaded the corridors, picking their way daintily over kitbags and recumbent, swearing figures, tinkling little gongs that summoned the ranks to multi-course breakfasts.

From that luxurious peak, the decline was rapid. The troops were transferred to the reality of the naval cruiser, *Devonshire* and then to the *Curacao*, scarcely larger than a destroyer. The *Devonshire* slipped away into the North Sea, there to be torpedoed and sunk.

During the voyage to Norway which, because of our zigzag course, took thirty-six hours, a German submarine drew a bead on the *Cedarbank*, the ship carrying all our transport and Bren carriers and neatly sank it. We were left to fight a campaign with Bren guns, rifles, revolvers and mortars with smoke shells but no high explosive, plus what we stood up in.

From Molde on the Norwegian coast we wound our way through silent fjords to Andalsnes on board a Norwegian coastal ferry whose captain spoke no English but whose radio was blaring Henry Hall and the BBC Dance Orchestra.

Elsewhere, the British radio and press were giving the impression that the German invasion had been checked, just north of Oslo, by the gallant Norwegian army, apart from the few Nazi parachutists dropped farther north, who were anyway said to be in the process of being mopped up.

Lies. The German mechanized columns were already roaring north, virtually unopposed a hundred miles from the capital.

We met them head on.

We were one of the few forces in modern times to go into battle in a train. This ancient contraption bore us through the frozen landscape to Lillehammer, southwest of Trondheim. There the expeditionary force, already exhausted from continuous travelling and with its transport at the bottom of the North Sea, transferred from the train to a haphazard assembly of Norwegian trucks. The convey slithered along mountain tracks beside the long, frozen finger of Lake Mjose. From the trucks we observed blue-clad figures lying in the snow, their unhelmeted heads and infrequent rifles pointing south. They waved us on, cheerily. "The brave British, come to defend us." We waved back.

The next thing we knew was that they had waved us straight into the Germans. A stream of tracer bullets ran up the road and onto the hood of the leading truck. The convoy halted; we scrambled for the trees, where we learned that the blue-clad figures were Norwegian infantry, weekend soldiers like ourselves, and even more ill-equipped.

During the first encounter, our Medical Officer reported two casualties: a man who had a headache, and a man who said he was frightened. They were shipped back to England.

The Air Liaison Officer put his foot down on Lake Mjose to test the strength of the ice for aircraft, and broke his ankle. He, too, was sent back to Blighty.

The rest of us peered fearfully through the trees, wondering what was going to come out of them. At eleven p.m. came the order to retreat. I still hadn't seen a German.

Overnight we slid in our army issue boots along the now icy mountain track to Lillehammer. The column became hopelessly jumbled. At dawn, some Norwegian trucks and private cars came to pick us up.

Unknown to us a German mechanized column had also moved overnight along a good parallel road, reaching Lillehammer first. There it awaited us. In fact, some of the Norwegian trucks drove a part of our force direct to the German headquarters. At that time, many Norwegians did not quite know whose side they were on. After a few months of German occupation they were no longer in doubt.

I was picked up by a large, fast civilian car which sped me through the suburbs and dropped me, shivering, at a point north of the city.

It was now the morning of Monday, April 22nd.

With a mixed collection of troops from other companies and battalions I crouched among the rocks in the April sun, gazing down at the road and the town and the lake below, waiting for the Germans to begin the next stage of their advance north. I had no binoculars; they had been stolen from my equipment earlier, by one of our own troops with a black market connection.

Reconnaissance planes began to circle above us. It was time to climb down the road, along which troops were now straggling north in a classic scene of retreat. Once off the road, it was impossible to move because of the waist-high snow and the terrain.

Among the stragglers was an officer of the Sherwood Foresters with whom I was acquainted. As we marched together beside abandoned trucks and ammunition cases, we spotted a bicycle. We tossed for it. He won, and my last sight of him was as he pedalled determinedly north.

Presently, the road led beside a frame house, in whose doorway stood one of my own men, eating calmly from a sardine tin as the retreat surged about him. "Luvly grub in 'ere, sir," he was saying when two large holes appeared in the walls of the house. There was a tremendous clatter from down the road towards Lillehammer. The troops began to run.

The sardine eater and I sprinted across the road to the shelter of a thick stone wall running alongside. There we crouched, as the racket increased and a tank rumbled past three feet from my head.

Thirty yards of waist-high snow separated us from the forest. As we ran for it there were shouts in German, and bullets spat into the mush around us. One of them hit the sardine eater; I reached the trees alone.

It was during this frantic dash that my revolver, which I had placed in my trouser pocket for safety, fell out. We had not been issued with the lanyards which were supposed to be attached to the ring on the butt. My steel helmet had also vanished during the debacle.

I was thus totally defenceless as I squatted beneath an overhanging boulder. On seeing us run, the entire German column had stopped, and had swarmed off the trucks and into the woods. They were all around us. It was not long before an extremely nervous German soldier, his rifle shaking as he pointed it at me, rounded the boulder and said, in English, " 'Ands 'oop."

I was immediately surrounded by camera-toting, English-speaking German non-commissioned officers, who took me down to the road and marched me with my hands up the whole length of the column, now back in its trucks and jeering. At a casualty clearing station I re-encountered the sardine eater. The German medicos, delighted to have a casualty to treat since they had none of their own, had already amputated what remained of his arm, bandaged the stump and placed him between sheets.

After marching back to Lillehammer with a few other early prisoners, we were soon joined by further victims of what Churchill later referred to as "this ramshackle campaign." Our numbers grew, and eventually we were trucked to Oslo, where I had what I hope will be my only experience of the inside of a civilian jail.

One of our number, a former school-teacher who spoke German, was taken to Berlin to meet Hitler. There, he was paraded on the lawn of the Chancellery, surrounded by captured equipment, including the notorious Boys anti-tank rifle, whose bullets were apt to bounce off anything thicker than cardboard. Hitler emerged, examined the equipment, snapped at the school-teacher, "It's your government who are responsible for this war," and stormed back into the Chancellery in a dreadful huff.

In Oslo, the rest of us boarded a steamer and were confined in the hold, only too mindful of the First Sea Lord's warning that he would "mine every ship in the Skaggerak and Kattegat." He must have missed us, for we reached the shelter of the Danish coast and eventually disembarked at what was then called Stettin. Our party of about twenty officers, under a single German guard, entrained for Berlin, which appeared in April 1940 to be on a peacetime footing. It was late afternoon rush hour when we arrived. Businessmen with briefcases first gaped then scoffed at us: "You have always wanted to visit Berlin. Well, now you are here."

While changing trains we lost our sentry, but eventually caught up with him. Where could we go, dressed as we were?

Where we eventually went was Spangenberg, a country-town set among the Hessian hills near the source of the River Weser, in which the Pied Piper of Hamelin drowned his rats. At this date, it embraced two small prison camps, the first in a former agricultural school consisting of several half-timbered blocks, and the other a traditional schloss, or castle, on a hill. In them were incarcerated the earliest prisoners: officers from the Royal Navy's *Glowworm* and the merchant ship *Rawalpindi,* and some airforce personnel who had been shot down in leaflet raids during the first days of the war. The latter included half-a-dozen Canadians who had been attached to the RAF. They had already prepared scrapbooks of their adventures, little

Oflag 1XA/H, Spangenberg, Lower Camp.
In the background is The Schloss, where French prisoners were housed during the
Napoleonic Wars. In the foreground, the bridge under which Tony Strachan escaped.

realizing that another five years lay ahead.

We were the first army group to be imprisoned at Spangenberg. I was allotted a number: P.O.W. 196.

The schloss had been used as a prison-camp throughout history. French prisoners from the Napoleonic Wars had scratched their names on the interior panelling, with the date: 1804. Although there was a military kommandant, the institution was run, as is often the case, by the janitor, a ferocious warlock named Kullmer who had lived there, we fancied, since before Charlemagne and who resented the intrusion of the twentieth century. The surrounding moat was inhabited by three wild boar, the neutered Gustav and two female companions to whom Gustav was therefore of little demonstrable use.

The invasion of Holland and Belgium, the capitulation of France, the blitz, the Battle of Britian — these were distant events of which we read in the German newspapers. Events which caused an influx of further prisoners whom the schloss was unable to hold. Army was separated from navy and airforce, and we were herded down into the camp in the town. There I spent hours discussing philosophy with

David Holland, later librarian at the House of Commons in London, and Airey Neave, a young barrister. At that time, it was quite in the cards that any one of us might meet a violent end. We could not have foretold that, forty years later, after a distinguished career culminating as right-hand man to British Prime Minister Margaret Thatcher, Airey Neave would be blown to pieces by an IRA bomb.

From this camp, David and I attempted to escape. The German quartermaster had an unlocked office adjacent to our *Speisesaal*, or dining-hall. Its floor contained a trapdoor leading to the foundations. For two weeks, we scraped with a kitchen knife around the mortar of a large foundation stone, loosening it.

On one occasion, as we were scraping, we heard someone enter the office and place an object on the trapdoor above us. It was, we recognized, a stepladder; a German painter had been roaming the camp, doing odd jobs. At that moment, the bell clanged for *appel* — a sudden, surprise check-parade. We were caught. If we stayed where we were, the roll-call would be two short, and a search would instantly be mounted.

David, who was six-feet-seven, placed his shoulders under the trapdoor and pushed. We had visions of the painter, on his stepladder, rising slowly to heaven. The trapdoor opened, the ladder toppled, minus painter. He had gone for a leak. We dashed onto the parade ground, breathless and late, and there received a reprimand from a major in the Guards.

I was now twenty.

In April 1941, Hitler, hearing the German prisoners were reputed to be confined below ground in Kingston, Ontario, where guards were also reputed to carry truncheons, decided on reprisals. With characteristic vengeful thoroughness he searched occupied Europe and discovered a series of forts constructed along the Russo-German frontier during one of those innumerable periods in history when Poland has ceased to exist.

There we were, indeed, confined below ground. And the guards did wear truncheons on their belts, though by the end of the first day only three were left; the rest had been pinched by prisoners creeping up behind the guards and removing them to keep as souvenirs.

That spring, from the earthworks on top of the fort, gazing across the river Vistula, we watched troop-trains rumbling eastward through Poland. Thus we learned, before most people, of the imminent invasion of Russia. Later, we saw the same trains returning, marked with hospital crosses.

It was in Poland that I celebrated my twenty-first birthday with a plate of porridge.

In the autumn, it was decided to move us farther from the battle zone, and we were transferred to Westphalia, via Berlin. I have visited Berlin five times in my life, each time in a cattle truck. On this occasion, when the train halted, David Holland poked his head out to see what was going on. There was a crack. A colleague looked up from his copy of Chaucer. "Was that a shot?" he asked. "Yes," replied David. "It was at me."

The camp in Westphalia perched on a windswept plain, where the temperature that winter sank to 48 degrees F below. We stuck cigarette butts in the chinks between the wall boards, to keep out the wind. Then we discovered the cellar where the Germans kept their coal supply. With the aid of a British orderly, an expert lock-picker whose peacetime trade had lodged him several times in jail, our warmth was henceforth assured.

Through one of those bureaucratic idiosyncracies which continue even in total war, an agreement had been reached under the Geneva Convention that our army wages would continue to be paid, two thirds to our credit in England, and one third in a special camp currency known as *Lagermarks*. There comes a time when the benefits of ersatz beer and mugs inscribed "A gift from Bavaria," begin to pall. We had now accumulated so many *Lagermarks* that the Senior British Officer offered to buy the camp, so that we could burn what we wanted and thus remain warm. The Germans made a counter offer: they would convert the *Lagermarks* into ordinary currency, and we could transfer it home. So we did, and bought a Spitfire with it. It is intriguing to think of our purchase taking potshots at the enemy, its fuselage painted with the words: "A gift from the boys of Oflag VI B."

It was in Westphalia that the message went out over the public-address system: "Has anybody got a spare pair of legs? Group-Captain Bader has broken his on the camp slide."

The story has it that when the legless air ace escaped and was recaptured, the guard tried to make him stand all night by hitting his legs with a rifle butt. The guard couldn't understand why Bader merely laughed. He didn't realize that the butt was merely striking against the artificial iron legs.

Here, too, we experienced our most hysterical kommandant, Rademacher, whom I once saw rip a British prisoner's tunic in revenge for his leaving an opened sardine tin teetering on a cupboard top so that, during a snap search, it fell and covered Rademacher's beautiful uniform with oil. The tunic was not on the Briton at the time, but on a coat hanger.

Rademacher had one weakness: he had played tennis at Wimbledon before the war. You had only to break in on one of his rages with "Von Cramm, Herr Kommandant! Bill Tilden! Bunny Austin!" and his hysteria would subside, his face wreathe in smiles. "Ah, yes. I well remember, during the second set, Fred Perry was at the net. . . "

The Russians in the neighbouring compound had no such avenue of appeasement. Most Allied prisoners were protected by the Geneva Convention, to which the Germans subscribed. (They knew that if we were mistreated the Allies had the power to take reprisals against German prisoners in the U.K. and Canada.) The Russians, on the other hand, were unprotected. There were two hundred of them in the compound. By the end of the first winter they were down to seventy-five, the others having died from malnutrition and disease. Their rations were a quarter of ours, and of course no Red Cross parcels. We used to chuck pieces of bread to them over the barbed wire while the sentries in the watchtowers took potshots at us. Some of them had been made to walk all the way to Germany from where they were captured deep in the heart of Russia. There were tales of cannibalism.

They used to come into our compound to be deloused in the showers. Wearing curious spiked woollen balaclava helmets, they had reached that pitch of emaciation where they looked like little children. They walked, infinitely slowly, between groups of British and Canadian prisoners who hurled abuse at their German escorts. But their spirits kept up, prodded by the Party agents in their midst. We could hear them singing revolutionary songs at night and, when a note of thanks for the bread was smuggled to us it contained phrases referring to "our glorious cause against the fascists."

Westphalia proved to be too near the Dutch border for our hosts. One month, during the summer of '42, there was an attempted escape every single night. So once again we were on the move, this time to the remoteness of Lower Bavaria and a town called Eichstatt, a prince-bishopric that contained, we were told, twenty-seven cathedrals. There we eked out our remaining two-and-a-half years.

There, too, there shortly appeared a piece of graffiti on the wall of the latrine: "*Premier essai* — Dieppe" — an inference that the battle of Dieppe was the first attempt to set up a second front in Europe. The prisoners from Dieppe began to turn up. Some of them had been placed in manacles after capture. (A German propaganda sheet in English misprinted the - a's, so that the printed version read "monocles.") On arrival at the camp they intermingled with the other residents, and in exasperation the Germans decided to isolate a whole block, Block One, behind extra barbed wire with all the inmates, Canadian or British, wearing manacles. Within five minutes it was discovered that the chains could be removed with the aid of a sardine key. The Germans then conceded that they need only be worn on check parade. Most prisoners did not even bother to do that, merely carrying the manacles and swinging them nonchalantly as their hosts tried to count them.

The senior medical officer, fearing that the inmates of Block One might suffer mental deterioration owing to isolation, received permission to make a tour of the block. The mission was supposed to be secret so that he could observe the inhabitants in their natural state. They got wind of his plan and, as he approached, they appeared at the windows, eyes rolling and voices crackling with maniacal laughter. He retreated in discomfort. Shortly afterwards the barbed wire was removed and the manacles withdrawn.

The question most commonly asked of ex-prisoners of war is: How were you treated? The glib answer would be that we weren't treated at all; we were on one side of the barbed wire, while our hosts were on the other. In fact, as British army officers, under the protection of the Wehrmacht, we came at the top of the treatment scale, whereas the concentration camps, under the SS, came at the bottom. (In the alphabet of treatment, if we were at the letter A, the Japanese prison-camps would be around a letter W.) Moreover, as officers, we were not obliged to work. Boredom, rather than privation, was our lot. Also in many instances, guilt. This may seem unreasonable in an era when a general could surrender an entire army and his troops had no option but to lay down their arms. Surely no fault could be attached, for example, to the aircraftsman who, on a bombing raid over Germany, when his captain turned and snapped a command, thought that he said "jump," opened the door and parachuted gently down to Bavaria? The captain had not said jump, he had something else, and the plane flew back to England minus one member of its crew. Fortunately for the aircraftsman's peace of mind the same plane was shot down on its next raid and its crew reunited in the same prison-camp. On welcoming his captain behind barbed wire the first words of the aircraftsman were: "I thought you said jump."

Nevertheless, there were those who felt ashamed at having been taken prisoner. They were usually officers of the regular armed forces who had been brought up in a tradition of "death rather than surrender." In fact one young man received a message to that effect from his father, who held senior rank in the army. "Never darken my door again," etc. Months later the young man burst into our hut brandishing a letter. "Guess what! The old man's been captured at Singapore."

How did the average officer prisoner occupy his time? There were four main pursuits: study, entertainment, exercise and escape.

After a year of incarceration, you become aware that this is not a gap in your life, it *is* your life, and you had better make the most of it. You accumulate things, starting with empty tins and bootlaces and gradually acquiring, through the Red Cross and other organizations, clothing, books, musical instruments, footballs and even skates. You become ingenious; you make things. A camp of two thousand contains people from all walks of life; not only professional warriors but also men who in peacetime were barristers, farmers, actors, musicians and mining engineers.

For the first time in their lives, many had an unlimited period in which to read and think. They studied. Examination papers were sent out from England and, with senior officers invigilating, prisoners became lawyers, accountants, company secretaries. In this respect they were luckier than many of their contemporaries who had not been captured.

On the entertainment side, when you realize that we had with us Michael Langham, who became director at the Stratford theatre, Ontario; Desmond Llewellyn, who later appeared in the James Bond movies and Rupert Davies, who became famous as Simenon's Maigret on BBC-TV, to

Prison camp production of Noel Coward's play *Post Mortem*. At right, Michael Langham later noted director of Stratford Festival in Ontario. Extreme left, Desmond Llewelym who played "M" in the James Bond movies.

name only three, it is hardly surprising that one of our productions, *Post Mortem*, achieved the distinction of a mention in Sheridan Morley's biography of Noel Coward. Eventually, we were renting costumes from the Munich State Opera which, at that juncture, had no use for them.

Authors, of course, abounded. Apart from the writers of best-selling escape stories, one who was to achieve prominence was David Walker, who later won the Governor-General of Canada Award for Literature.

In music we ranged from a bassoonist with the London Philharmonic to an American who had played bass for Bunny Berrigan, from orchestras capable of performing the easier symphonies, such as Schubert's Fifth, to jazz combos echoing *In the Mood*.

Eichstatt had been a barracks, so there was a football field with wooden seats set in a bank to form a primitive grandstand. We dug and banked smaller recreational areas where, when the earth baked hard in the summer, we played five-a-side field hockey. In winter, we flooded them laboriously, using tea urns, to a depth of a few inches, then skated on them. Half-a-dozen pairs of skis arrived; we flopped enthusiastically down the banks. Canadians taught ice-hockey, wielding sticks and pucks sent via Switzerland.

In none of this did our hosts interfere. A camp of two thousand enemy prisoners, set in the civilian countryside, is potentially explosive. The Germans gradually became aware that the more contented the prisoner the less incentive he had to cause trouble, the less likely he was to try to escape.

The flaw was that officers, under King's Regulations, were under an obligation to attempt to break out. Nevertheless, the practice did not at the time achieve the prominence it later attained in literature and movies. Escapers, their wild eyes glinting from earth-covered heads that suddenly popped up between the floorboards of a hitherto placid classroom studying Greek, were a disturbing influence, and not only to the Germans. Even so, I suppose that every prisoner who was in for as long as five years had at least one shot at it, or was at least involved in assisting others.

The first attempt occurred at the schloss in Spangenberg. Two German house-painters in white coats entered the camp, put down a ladder and disappeared into a building. A few minutes later, two Canadian airmen, dressed in white coats they had made from sheets, emerged from a doorway, picked up the ladder, went to the main gate and were let out. When the real painters reappeared and could not find their ladder, the alarm was raised. The two escapers were detected on a road leading to the countryside, were brought back to the guardhouse and beaten up.

At Warburg, in Westphalia, the business became more sophisticated. The mining engineers got to work. They ran electricity off the main circuit so that tunnels were illuminated. Roof supports were constructed from bedboards, and little railways were made from tins to bring the earth back from the face. So many tunnels were dug under one hut that it began to sink into the ground.

The entrance to another tunnel lay in the open, in the middle of a vegetable garden, covered by a shallow, soil-covered tray. When the guard in the watchtower was looking the other way, you lifted the tray and presto! — down you went.

On one memorable evening we fused the perimeter lights, and the camp was pitched in darkness. Out of the huts rushed two dozen prisoners bearing hinged ladders, again made from bedboards — one length of ladder to go up the barbed wire and the other to go across the top, so that the fugitives could jump down the other side.

The Germans adopted various measures to counter these shenanigans. They loosed savage guard dogs in the compound at night; the prisoners tamed the dogs with tit-bits from Red Cross parcels. After a few nights an inmate secured his particular pet, took it to the main gate and claimed to be a shepherd who had lost his dog which apparently had wandered into the camp. Now that he had found it, could he please be let out?

On another occasion, a prisoner dressed himself in what he imagined to be Ottoman garb, plastered with half moons made from cigarette foil. Accompanied by the camp's female impersonator, who wore a yashmak, he presented himself at the main gate and identified himself as the Turkish ambassador. Most interesting visit, now regrettably over. Might they now be permitted to leave?

Our hosts were not deceived, but they felt it advisable to transfer us to Bavaria. There they were duped by the greated hoax of all.

A German general, with his entourage, decided to visit the camp. He completed his tour of inspection and, after three hours, was duly let out. Half-an-hour later, another German general appeared at the main gate, demanding to leave.

The guard refused, wagged his finger at him. "I know you Pritish! You are always choking." The general began to swear. Presently, as it dawned on the guard that no mere Briton could swear so fluently in German, he realized his gaffe. *"Mein General, es tut mir leid* — I am sorry." Meanwhile the bogus general, with his small group, was already legging it over the Bavarian fields.

Fortune smiled less favourably on three young fighter pilots who escaped in the hope of finding a plane and flying it home. Disguised in made-up German airforce uniforms they located an airfield and there, on a runway, lay the very plane they were seeking. They made for it, their pace quickening. A voice bellowed. Turning, they saw a senior *feldwebel*. They veered away from him. The voice bellowed again. One of them had learnt one German phrase: *"Ein Moment — ich komm zuruck in zwei Minuten"* ("hang on — I'll be back in two minutes.") It is not the sort of thing you say to a senior *feldwebel*, who is the equivalent of a regimental sergeant-major in the Brigade of Guards. The *feldwebel* swelled like a frog. *"Ein Moment?"* he repeated, unable to believe his ears. He placed them under close arrest. When, unable to speak German except for the offending phrase, they remained silent, he had them up before his commanding officer on a charge of dumb insolence. Only later was it discovered that they were prisoners of war.

From all these attempts, probably half-a-dozen made it back to England. Any ex-kriegy will tell you that it is not too difficult to get out of a camp. It's once you're out that the real trouble begins.

When David Holland and I escaped — two extraordinary figures, one six-feet-seven and the other a foot shorter, flitting at midnight over the cobbles of Spangenberg — we were apprehended almost at once. The bunker where we were to spend our regulation solitary confinement was already full, so we had to wait our turn. The last man on the list decided that he liked the peace and solitude so well that, when his turn was up, he refused to leave and turned the cell into his private room, lined with Red Cross books and bedecked with flowers stolen from the Kommandant's wife's garden.

Thus captives throughout history turn the rigours of confinement to advantage — like the German POW in Canada who, immigrating after the war, tried to use his period behind barbed wire as a residency qualification when applying for Canadian citizenship.

In order to detect tunnels the Germans procured a metal diviner. Proudly brandishing their new toy, they entered a hut, where one of them put down some wire-cutters on a stool as they commenced their search. The cutters were immediately snapped up by a kriegy and shoved under a straw mattress. The search continued. Suddenly, the metal-diviner began to vibrate. "Ah! A tunnel!" They pulled back a mattress and revealed — their own wire cutters.

Once, in desperation, they decided to put an end to all this nonsense. After check parade one morning they detained us on the parade ground. The camp gates swung to and, three abreast, clad in homburgs and long black raincoats and clutching briefcases, hordes of plainclothes Gestapo marched in. At once the assembled kriegies broke into the Policeman's March. Rum-te-tum, rum-te-tum. Further and more pronounced irreverence continued throughout the day's search. At the end of it Himmler's dreaded force was in shambles, with briefcases missing, papers mixed up, and hats pinched as souvenirs. Some were in tears. They never visited us again.

Further efforts to dictate the lives of POW's went similarly awry. On one occasion the authorities, mindful of racial purity and full of Teutonic logic, conceived the idea of confining the Jews and the Arabs in the same hut. "After all, both are semitic. They are non-Aryan." Three days later the hut exploded, with bits of Jew and Arab being scattered to the winds of Westphalia.

What about sex? The question may be answered best

by reference to the memoirs of a First World War prisoner who was confined in a camp of mixed nationalities. "The French," he wrote, "slept with silk stockings under their pillows. The Poles had women smuggled in dressed as orderlies. The British stood and threw heavy balls about." Nevertheless, in the early days, one young RAF officer had scrawled on the wall above his bed: "Home or homo by Christmas."

When he can't get sex, a man may turn to another prop, booze. We could buy a sort of beer in the canteen, and attempts were made to brew a camp hooch by soaking dried raisins and figs in a metal container and distilling the result by drawing it up through a pipe to a kettle perched on a table. At one memorable camp concert when Major Cloutier's version of "Alouette" received a sitting ovation, two prisoners who had been imbibing went into convulsions and were carried to hospital. Fortunately for the health of the inmates, the Germans usually found the tubs of hooch on their snap searches and emptied them in the snow. So we did better things with the raisins and figs, like eating them.

What, then, was the worst aspect of captivity for the officer prisoner? "By far the most unpleasant discomfort of a prison camp," wrote Captain Robin Campbell, D.S.O., in the magazine *Horizon*, "was the lack of privacy." Referring to the twenty feet square "bed-sitting room" in which he lived, ate, slept, sweated and swore with fifteen others, he mentioned that "the longest period I was alone in that room was eighteen minutes. To become adapted to this lack of solitude it was necessary to develop a kind of reptilian insensitivity — like crocodiles in their tank at the zoo, which walk over each other without either appearing to notice the other."

By the summer of 1944, even Bavaria was insufficiently remote. We could see the Allied bombing fleets, tiny silver fish in the azure, droning their way to Augsburg. Our guards became progressively more decrepit and more corruptible, as the Eastern front took its toll. "Russki Komm," we used to taunt them. On the whole they were amiable old men. We bribed them with cigarettes and bought a goose for Christmas.

In January of the new year, Germany crumbled. By April Allied forces had penetrated deep into the Fatherland; their airforces had demolished the first-class roads and railways, and we were now concentrating on the second-class. This fact was on our minds as the Germans moved us for the last time, to a camp south of the Danube, thus placing the river between us and the liberating armies. On this forced march, we were guarded by Volksturm, the German Dad's Army, who were so moth-eaten that we carried their rifles for them.

While marching through the open country outside Eichstatt, we were strafed by American rocket-firing Typhoon aircraft, their pilots presumably imagining that a moving column must be enemy. When our Allies were done with us, forty old-time POWs lay dead. Eric Arden, in peacetime a professional pianist, had his arm shot off — like my own sardine eater five years previously.

Our final camp, Moosberg, was a hellhole containing fourteen thousand British and sixteen thousand Americans. Luckily we had to remain there only three weeks as Patch's Seventh and Patton's Third U.S. Armies raced across Bavaria towards us. We knew they were coming — we had secret radios in abundance, smuggled in by newcomers over the years. (After one search, when thirty-three radios were discovered by the Germans, there still remained enough for our purposes.)

Inevitably Patton won the race. The German kommandant drove out to meet him. "I command a large area full of prison-camps." he said. "There is typhus. If you will declare it neutral territory, I will hand it over to you intact."

"Balls," replied Blood-and-Guts. "The battle begins at dawn."

It was all over in twenty minutes. The first we knew

Prisoners are freed by US Army units   **(US Army Photo).**

that we had been liberated was when the main gate crashed open and a Sherman tank rumbled down the Lagerstrasse, the camp's main street. All the Americans who had been prisoners for five weeks, rushed about getting souvenirs, while the British who had been prisoners five years, lay on their beds and read books. Finally, one of them put aside his copy of Plato. "I suppose," he murmured, "that we're technically free." He resumed his reading. It was the 29th of April, 1945.

Apart from freedom, the first relief our liberators brought to us was a machine for making doughnuts. This was greeted with ecstatic whoops by the GIs. I preferred hard tack biscuits, and had completed some brisk trading in this commodity when I ducked under a tent flap and bumped against the broad bottom of General Patton himself. And yes, he did wear pearl-handled revolvers, and did look capable of slapping my face.

For the period, camp life continued much as before, except that things were less well run by the Americans than they had been by the Germans. Much of our time was spent preventing liberated Russian prisoners from raping ancient German crones. Roger Mortimer, a captain in the Coldstream Guards who later became racing correspondent for the London *Sunday Times,* came up to me and said, "The artificial life we laboriously built up over five years has collapsed. I'm *dreading* going home."

But go home we did, a few days later. U.S. airforce Dakotas flew us to a base in Oxfordshire where the army authorities, bureaucratic somnolence disturbed by the influx of returned kriegies, tried to sort us out. We had to fill in a form; one of the questions asked, "Do you know anyone who committed treason while a prisoner of war?" Some malcontents wrote the names of people who owed them money from the card tables, then hastened to the canteen. Our first meal consisted of underdone roast pork — it was the ration for the British army on that particular day and, from the caterer's viewpoint, a thing like dysentery could go hang.

I returned to England on the day the war in Europe ended — two days before my twenty-fifth birthday and five years and three weeks after I had landed in Norway.

We were given some tickets, shoved on a train and told to make our own way home. Arriving at a country station in Leicestershire I phoned my mother, who used valuable petrol coupons to come and fetch me. Her voice sounded oddly high and squeaky. I thought she had a cold. Then I realized I had not heard a woman's voice for five years.

Two short months later I was back in the army, being trained for the invasion of Japan, which fortunately surrendered before I could get there. I remained in the army until July, 1946. I had started as a second-lieutenant and ended, seven years later, as a first-lieutenant. All my contemporaries who had not been captured were either generals or dead. Thus if there is any lesson to pass to another generation, it is this: Never join up young. If you do, they've got you and, by God, they'll keep you.

8

Drop Over Utrecht

Jim Lang

from a taped interview

It was Sunday, October 11th, 1942. I was a Flying Officer pilot attached to 105 Squadron, stationed at Marham in Norfolk, England. My observer, Flying Officer Tommy Thomas, D.F.C. and myself were scheduled to carry out a Met' reconnaisance flight over Germany to gather information for Bomber Command, who would be operating in force that night.

On arriving at the crew room at 10 a.m. we were informed that the operation had been 'scrubbed' and that the squadron would be on stand-down for the next forty-eight hours.

As we were due for a week's leave Tommy and I made several telephone calls, looked up train schedules, etc. and were all set to leave Kings Lynn that evening. At approximately 1 p.m. however, a message over the tannoy system advised six crews, including ours, to report to the Op's Room at once. I located Tommy in the squash courts, alerted him and waited for him to change before we were able to report. We were the last crew to get to the briefing and were advised that three separate boxes of two planes were to fly to Hanover to bomb the city at dusk. There were three different routes selected. Being late, we were to take the one entering enemy territory at the Zuider Zee, the least popular one. Squadron-Leader Jimmy Knowles, who had earned a D.F.C. on a tour of shipping strikes in the English Channel on Blenheims, had just come off a rest period, and this was to be his first 'Op' on a Mosquito. I was to follow him in loose formation to the target, flying at thirty thousand feet on a course that would take us to the Zuider Zee, where we would change course to Hanover.

The Mosquito was at this time still on the secret list and 105 Squadron was the first squadron to fly it in Bomber Command. I know now that we were testing the operational qualities of the airplane, flying photographic reconnaissance, meteorological reconnaissance, low-level strikes, high-level nuisance raids, etc. We carried four two hundred and fifty lb. bombs; had no guns, relying mostly on our speed and height (to be the most effective). Flying singly on most missions, Tommy and I were one of five of the original twenty crews left who began operating that summer; two planes having taken part in the first one-thousand plane raid on Cologne, to start things off for the newly formed 105 squadron.

We took off from the aerodrome at 1641 hours, climbing rather erratically owing to the difficulty in trying to retain some form of formation with Jimmy, who I was following. We lost valuable time getting to our first change of course.

In the past, crews had not been intercepted on the way in to the target, as a general rule — because of our height, speed and surprise, the fighter squadrons did not get high enough, early enough before we crossed the Dutch coast — but today was to be an exception (and we were to be the victims).

As we saw the Zuider Zee ahead of us, Tommy was

giving me a new course to fly to the target when there was an enormous explosion; the aircraft shuddered, and I was no longer able to keep the plane straight and level. Having wondered for many months what it would feel like to be hit by enemy fire, there was no doubt in our minds that this was it! The ailerons no longer responded and I had lost control of the aircraft.

I shouted at Tommy to get out. He climbed to the nose of the plane where the bomb sight was, collected his parachute, and proceeded to carry out the procedures of bailing out. In the meantime, we were hit a second time with cannon shells setting the starboard engine on fire and throwing the airplane into a drunken attitude, trying madly to turn over on its back; I, not too effectively, doing all I could to prevent it. Tommy was able to get out through the floor hatch during the panic that was going on. I jettisoned the narrow hood above me, released the straps which held me in my seat, took off my helmet and oxygen mask — not really knowing in that short time what was going to happen next, or why I was doing what I was.

I really had nowhere to go, since I could not get across to the floor hatch because the stick was in my way. I was awkward with my seat-pack and dinghy attached and certainly could not get through the hatch to drop out. Also the hood above me was too narrow for me to get through under normal, on-the-ground circumstances, let alone in the plane I was trapped in, now spinning out of control. The third attack, thank God, was only a near miss. I had never seen so many cannon-shells exploding around me; I certainly never hope to again. I can only imagine that the German pilot of that FW190 got a little over-anxious when he found us going down in a sitting-duck position.

My next recollection was, in all probability, the most memorable experience of my life. I was suspended alive, in mid-air, my parachute supporting me. I was unhurt — it was terribly cold — my watch was still going, and I had somehow lost approximately five minutes that I will never be able to account for. Amazingly enough, I have no recollection of pulling my ripcord, and the handle was not in my hand when I regained consciousness (the mystery remains unsolved). Perhaps my memory had suffered due to a lack of oxygen when I removed my mask earlier. I have had nightmares for years where I have been trapped, my arms and legs being pinned, and perhaps somewhere during that lost time in that incredibly narrow space, I did things I was not aware of. Whatever those things were I will never know, but they must have been the right ones to allow me to talk about them now. How did I ever get out of the airplane, and how was the ripcord of my parachute pulled? I am still very happy to believe it was a miracle.

Twenty minutes later I hit the ground just outside the city of Utrecht. The time spent on the parachute I like to refer to as my most exciting journey ever because, in spite of the eerie feeling of being surrounded by cloud with no sensation of falling, for part of the trip, I had time to think about what had happened — how fortunate I was to be alive and how I must get myself prepared for what was going to happen next.

It was awfully quiet in the field I landed in, with little canals on either side of me. I almost expected all hell to break loose, people to appear, Germans to be there waiting for me — but it was not to be. I was not at all sure what I was going to do as it was late evening and would be dark quite soon. I hid my dinghy and parachute in a ditch and decided to walk across to a barn which was about half a mile away to try to decide what in the hell to do. On the way across the field, between myself and the barn, was a gate and, surprisingly enough, an old man was leaning on it smoking a pipe. I walked up to him and tried to signify that I was a pilot, pointing to my wings; that I had been shot down and could he help me? Of course he could not understand a word I said, but I must say, I did not quite expect such a total lack of interest. He gave no indication that I was even addressing him. He certainly said nothing to acknowledge me, continuing to puff on his pipe, perhaps letting me know that he had no wish to become involved. I walked on to the barn, climbed into the loft, lay down on the straw to try to get my thinking straight.

After a while I heard voices, and gathered I was being called down to identify myself. I later learned I had been spoken to in German. There were three civilians standing there. One of them addressed me in English, to which I replied, "Are you Deutsch?" The answer left no doubt in my mind that the "deutscher" was no good — that they were Netherlanders, and that they were pleased to meet me and intended to help me. I shook them all warmly by the hand, seldom being as pleased to see anyone as I was to see them. The oldest man of the group told me that he lived in Utrecht, that he was going to take me to a place approximately a mile away where I would be given a rain-coat and a bicycle to ride. I was to follow him, not any closer than two hundred yards — just far enough away to keep them in sight. I was to ride the bicycle following the group into Utrecht at about the same distance. He was tak-ing me to his home. His instructions were: "When you get to the house following us, knock on the door, the light will go out, the door will open. It will be dark but walk through the door and shut it. My wife will be there and I would like you to introduce yourself. I will follow a few minutes later once you are inside." I did as I was told and arrived at the house without incident other than passing a group of German soldiers returning to barracks singing "Roll out the Barrel", and almost running down a German patrol in the streets of Utrecht unwittingly saying "whoops — sorry" and getting away with it!

There were six people in the living-room, the man and his wife who owned the house, the two young men who had met me at the barn earlier, and another man and his wife, Jewish people who had been turned out of their house next door to provide a German officers' mess. How brave these people were, how friendly and anxious to do all they could to help! It was such a contrast to the events of a few hours earlier. Plans were made to take me to a cabin approximately three miles away in the country, close to the circuit of Soesterberg aerodrome. Once again I followed one of the young Dutchmen on my borrowed bicycle arriving at our destination just before darkness fell.

For nearly a week I lived there undisturbed other than daily visits from one of my new friends to bring me food, and an update on their frantic efforts to get me out of the country. The day before I had to leave this location I spent a most memorable afternoon sitting in the sunshine outside the cabin having tea and biscuits with my delightful Dutch hosts. They were, I believe, genuinely sorry to let me go to attempt to find my way alone.

I left my refuge on a wet, cold, depressing Sunday evening and I was picked up during the curfew by a Dutch policeman, after wandering through the outskirts of Utrecht. He immediately took me to the local police station where I was again received with handshakes and pats on the back, but, at the same time, warned that I was to be turned over to the German authorities.

After about fifteen minutes of amicable conversation, the scene changed. In the street, outside the station, there was a roar of sirens; a cavalcade of cars and motorcycles, several German soldiers in helmets and full battle regalia, tommy-guns and rifles, entered the room and surrounded us; closely followed by a Prussian officer complete with cape, ceremonial dress and sword, who entered with much flourish. I was apprehensive as he cursed two Dutch policemen who failed to stand up as he came in, but he then saluted me and indicated that I was his prisoner.

Squashed between two German soldiers in the back seat of a car, with the German officer in the front seat, I was next driven with full motorcycle escort, sirens blaring, through the streets to what I learned later was back to the aerodrome at Soesterberg. Arriving there, I was handed over to an English-speaking German major complete with an Iron

Cross from the First World War, who took me into his office in the mess, poured me a drink of Johnny Walker scotch, and proceeded to question me about my situation — how I had arrived in DeBilt, how long I had been there, whether I had had any assistance from the Dutch people. Whether he associated me with my airplane, which had crashed in the vicinity a week earlier, I will never know. He appeared to be more interested in telling me that he had made many trips to England in peacetime from Bremen and knew the English well. He bragged about the successes of the Germans to date in France, Belgium and Holland, as well as Rommel's forces in North Africa, but my interview could not in any way have been considered the form of interrogation I had anticipated.

That night was spent in the aerodrome jail in a cell where I met several Luftwaffe personnel, prisoners for various discipline offences. Our remarks to one another were cordial, no real animosity being shown, and I gathered that they would have liked to question me about a lot of things but owing to our language difficulties we never got past the frau-and-kinder, wife-and-family type of conversation.

Herr Major collected me the next morning and drove me by car to Rotterdam where he put me on a train to Amsterdam with two guards as escort. He saluted me "goodbye" and wished me "good luck" in the next stage of my life as a kriegsgefangener. At Amsterdam I was taken by bus to the famous Amsterdam jail, remaining there for four days until I was taken from my cell and escorted to the railway station for the next train-ride, this time to Frankfurt-am-Main. An Australian pilot who had been in hospital for a month in Amsterdam and two guards were to be my companions down the Rhine for the next twenty-four hours.

The Aussie understood some German and we must have talked the whole night through because there was little opportunity to sleep under the circumstances. We passed

Dulag holding unit and transit camp for interrogation of newly captured prisoners.
(US Army Photo)

through Cologne in the early hours of the morning and I remember it being pointed out by our guards that the city was not really as badly damaged as our newspapers had claimed after the first one-thousand plane raid that summer. One incident I remember well as being most unexpected — a German woman ticket-collector on the train during the night joined us in our carriage and was most curious about us. She asked many questions of the guards and my fellow passenger, but when she left us at five o'clock in the morning, she passed two cigarettes to each of us, said goodbye and wished us well.

On arrival at Frankfurt we were taken to the Dulag Luft interrogation centre for airforce prisoners, on the outskirts of Wiesbaden. Once more into the cells for twenty-four hours when interrogation began in earnest.

Our treatment was not at all pleasant. The guards made our life as difficult as they could. Our clothes were taken away from us for twelve hours and the heating system was turned on and off with great frequency. I awoke in the middle of the night, lying on the floor, alongside the door, almost unconscious, struggling for breath. The cell was quite airless and hot. Eventually it was my turn to be sent to the main assembly camp where I would finally meet other air crew, before being sent further into Germany to Stalag Luft III. Here I finally caught up to my Observer, Tommy, who had a wonderful tale to tell. When he bailed out at twenty-nine thousand feet he had fallen at least twelve-thousand feet before he was able to clip his chest pack to his parachute straps to enable him to pull the ripcord. He probably hit the ground ten minutes before I did, fell into a moat, and was taken prisoner at once.

As this camp was a transit camp, it was another week before there were enough of us to make up a train-load for the long trip to Sagan. It was good to feel relatively settled among other air crew at last after being alone for so long, not knowing what the business of being a prisoner-of-war was leading to. If my twenty-minute ride to the ground from twenty-nine thousand feet was the most memorable one of my life, I believe that the next two days and nights, sitting upright in a third-class railway carriage, with fifty or sixty others, was a close second. Closely-guarded, with little or no food, we became a very demoralized group — but together, we survived the journey and arrived at Sagan in the early morning.

We got our first view of the famous Stalag Luft III, the large barbed wire enclosure, with the raised sentry boxes and searchlights. At approximately 7:30 that morning a large, cheerful, red-faced, Squadron-Leader, Jennings, the Camp Adjutant, greeted us and led us through the various protective wire enclosures into the main camp. We struggled through the main gate and were greeted by a crowd of prisoners; some who had been there since September 1939, some perhaps only a few weeks, but all anxious to look us over to see whether they would know anyone and to get the latest news from England. Each one of us was intercepted and escorted to a room, in one of the blocks in the camp, by another prisoner, given a "brew" and asked questions that would enable them to identify us as genuine aircrew.

And so began a life behind barbed wire — the life of a kriegie, as a guest of the Third Reich, for two and one-half years between October, 1942, and May, 1945.

9

Birthday In Buchenwald

Bill Gibson

from a taped interview

I was flying tailgunner on a Lancaster Bomber on my eleventh trip, July 4th, 1944. After seven fighter attacks, a Junker 88 shot us down. We bailed out; the whole crew of seven got out alive and contacted the French Underground who passed us on to various farms until finally we were driven to Paris. We should have became suspicious because cars weren't that plentiful in France, gasoline being very scarce.

We were lodged in a hotel where we stayed a week, and a so-called Resistance man kept calling on us two or three times a day, telling us we were going to start our journey towards the Pyrenees and Spain. We believed him because he was very sincere about it. He told us that at a quarter to five one evening they would be picking us up and starting our journey south. We went downstairs, out of the side door of the hotel, and got into a big black car which was equipped with secondary gas tanks in the back seat. We drove down the Champs Elysees, under the Arc

de Triomphe, where we made a sharp right turn. I saw
Swastika flags and two guards and felt something in my
ribs. I looked down — it was a 45 automatic. The guard
said, "Sorry, boys, German police. You are my prisoners."
So we got out of the car and saw the SS lined up with Sten
guns. We were taken to Gestapo headquarters and interrogated. There was a little humour because the interrogating
officers were a Frenchman who couldn't speak English and
a German who couldn't speak French.

After about an hour's interrogation, they called us
saboteurs and gangsters and terrorists because we were in
civilian clothes with no identification. They locked us up
in cells the size of telephone booths, two of us handcuffed
back to back. We were there for a day and then they put
us in travelling cells, little cabins, on trucks and took us
to a French prison where I stayed thirty-two days in solitary
confinement.

On the 19th of August they decided that they would
move us out of Paris. We'd no idea where we were going.
They loaded us on the trains which were "forty-eights,"
made for forty soldiers or eight horses. We left Paris, the
whole crew in one car.

On the second night my pilot escaped with five Frenchmen by lifting the floorboards of the train and dropping
down between the wheels. The guards saw them and shot
them. They stopped the train, called us out and wanted to
know who the Englishmen in the trains were. There were
only seven of us, the rest of my crew and three people from
Jersey. They were going to shoot seven for each one that
escaped. Instead, they removed our clothes, took all our
food and water away from us and locked us in the car. There
were ninety-six men in the car meant for forty.

The following day there was a young boy who put his
hand on a window, which was quite high up. They fired
a shot at him through his hand, stopping the train again,
opened the door and hollered in, "Are you English or
French?"

We said, "French."

They told him to come out. He got out of the car and they told him to run and, when he started to do so, they opened fire, hit him in the back and killed him.

The train was strafed by Allied aircraft and the engine was shot out. We had to get out of the car, walk around and get on another train on the other side of town. Then we arrived at Buchenwald.

None of us knew what a concentration camp was; we'd never heard of one. We weren't off the train twenty minutes when the man next to me, an American, got hit in the face with a rifle butt because he didn't move fast enough. That was our first encounter with the SS in a concentration camp. We walked in through the gates with the wording above: "Arbeit Macht Frei" and were taken down to the showers and shaved completely — every bit of hair on our heads. Our clothes were taken away from us. We were issued with a cotton shirt and a pair of cotton pants and a number. My number was 78394.

They had no barracks to put us in and we slept on the side of a mountain for eight days. The Americans bombed the camp about five days after we got there and we were threatened with execution. We were called to the main square. I was so sure that I was going to die that day that I gave my food ration to a Frenchman. Our ration, incidentally, was a cup of mint tea for breakfast, a half inch of bread and half litre of soup and maybe two little potatoes for lunch, and a cup of coffee made from acorns for supper. So that day I gave mine to a Frenchman, saying, "I won't be needing it." I went up to the main square and there the Kommandant said, "You people made all this damage, you must clean it up." He asked each and every one of us what we did in civilian life; we were all instructed to say, "Nothing." He commented, "I have one hundred and sixty-seven hoboes," and that's exactly what he had because we did nothing. I remember two of us carried one bench around the camp all afternoon, and that was all we cleaned up.

They gave us crepe paper bandages and iodine to help the Russian wounded working in the factories, making parts for the V-1's; they were kept in the factories when the bombs came down. The SS machine-gunned anybody who tried to get out of the factory. There were twenty-two SS killed in the raid, and some of their families too, so they weren't too pleasant towards us.

We were sent back to where we were staying and finally got into a barracks, originally built for two hundred and fifty people and now holding six hundred. The interior was made up of ledges in five foot sections. Five prisoners lay in each section. We had fleas, lice, scabies, and dysentery. There was also typhoid and typhus in the camp.

Three thousand German Gypsy children were brought in, castrated and executed. Jews were also executed. I had a last meal with quite a few of them.

Two questions have been in my mind for forty years.

One is: Why were we put there? And the other: However did we get out of there?

One day we were called to the square where they executed people by strangulation and stabbings. There was an officer of the German Airforce whose first words to us, in English, were, "According to Geneva Convention, if you attempt to escape you will be shot." It was ironical for the Germans to be telling us this when we shouldn't have been there in the first place.

We were a sorry bunch. I think we may have lived about another two or three weeks if we had stayed.

I celebrated my nineteenth birthday there, on the 28th of September, 1944. It wasn't much of a celebration. In fact, it went by without my remembering. We left Buchenwald in October and arrived at Stalag Luft III, an airforce prisoner-of-war camp. When the Colonel saw us get off the train he asked us where we came from and was told, "Buchenwald concentration camp," and he said, "Camps like that don't exist in Germany."

The older I get the more my prisoner-of-war experiences affect me. In fact, I'm going up for my fourth pensions board very shortly. I've had three since being back, for a nervous condition. Each was turned down with the wording that it was a pre-enlistment ailment not aggravated by wartime service. I find this very difficult because if I had a nervous condition I would not have been accepted into the service, and would not have passed the aircrew medical; they certainly wouldn't have had me as a tailgunner protecting six other guys' lives if I had been a nervous wreck.

I've been going to psychiatrists for the last two years because I had been on drugs, barbiturates, ever since the war. I'm off those now. I showed them a letter from the Department of Veterans Affairs where I had a friend, a pensions advisor, who said, "Do you want me to open your case again?"

I said, "You do what you want."

He said, "If you can get any evidence from the doctor

that your condition has worsened, we would take it and use it."

I get very nervous. In the first year I was home, I could not sleep at night. I worked at night and would sleep in the daytime. For thirty years I couldn't sleep at night without a light on. A psychiatrist who teaches at Dalhousie University has dug up four reports on concentration camp inmates and has sent copies to the Department of Veterans Affairs. I asked him, "Do I have any symptoms that these investigations have shown?"

And he replied, "Yes, you have."

They include anxiety, panic, and morbidity — I'm terrified of dying. We saw death in some horrible ways. These things frighten me and I'm not ashamed to say it. Every morning I'm scared when I wake up. I get through the day fine. I know another chap who tells me it's in the afternoons that he's scared. I think we all of us have a psychiatric reaction to those years.

I'm on one hundred percent disability pension from Britain for hearing loss that was put down by a DVA doctor to malnutrition and lack of vitamins. Britain, although they're tough, seem to be much easier on pension disabilities.

I have found, and other people have found, that it's very difficult to have people believe you; that you were there and those things happened.

10

Korea

Jim King

We consisted of twenty-four officers and men of the British 29th Brigade, P.O.W.'s under Chinese control, captured during the battle of Imjim River, April 25th, 1951; now a sorry-looking bunch of ragged, gaunt and bearded scarecrows having marched, Lord knows where, backwards and forwards, up and down North Korea for seven weeks.

All our inquiries about our destination had been met with "mamandy" or the Chinese for "soon" or "in a little while". We had stumbled blindly along, on each others heels, over mountains and rivers and had passed through several small towns in darkness. We had experienced our own aircraft's low-level bombing and napalming and had been scared to death, but we believed we were headed for our own idealized version of a prisoner-of-war compound such as all had seen in the movies like *The Great Escape* where we would at last come to the end of our hike and be treated as human beings again with food that we could eat and medical treatment for our dysentery. Above all we would be able to get a bath, clean clothes and get

rid of the lice. Little did we guess what we would find at
our journey's end and what was to be our home from which
we never strayed more than a mile in any direction for the
next twenty-five months.

We were there before we even realized it, halted in
the middle of a big bare field, a heap of exhausted young
soldiers. Our usual squad of guards disappeared and some
comparatively clean, uniformed Chinese youths surrounded
us and stood warily. They seemed under the circumstances
comical with their oversized rifles and bayonets. To all our
inquiries and requests for food, water and shade, for it was
very hot, impassive grunts and waving of bayonets were
the only response. After several hours an older officer arrived, accompanied by an intellectual-looking Chinese who
called us to attention. We stood up and he then proceeded to harangue us in Chinese for what seemed like hours,
about how fortunate we criminals were to be allowed to
live and even be fed and sheltered by the followers of
China's Mao Tse Tung. He worked himself into such a rage
that we expected him to have a fit. At intervals, his buck-
toothed assistant stammered out elementary, though
threatening, phrases in broken English: "You running dogs
and imperialist warmongers."

We were soon to get used to similar daily and nightly
episodes in which, although the person who delivered the
harangue might change, the subject matter remained the
same, the eternal theme being that we killers of Korean
children and rapers of women were only allowed to live
this gracious life by the lenient policy of the Chinese
Peoples' Volunteers.

Eventually we were allowed into the Korean village
which was to be our open prison where our earlier hopes
were dashed and we immediately became less optimistic
about the Shangri-la we had dreamed of. The camp was
a fair-sized Korean village consisting of mud and wattle
walled houses with straw roofs. The walls were papered,
in some cases, with newspaper; the floors were dirt and

there was no furniture whatsoever.

The sights that bothered us most were the occasional glimpses of the walking dead: Belsen-victim types in the next block down the street, about one-hundred yards away. As soon as we could we found out what the drill was from the already existing inhabitants of the cottage we were assigned to. These were American marine P.O.W.'s who had in fact been there only a few days. The Korean civilians who had previously lived there had departed a few weeks before the place was commandeered. The neighbours down the road were Americans unfortunate enough to have been captured six months earlier in the depths of winter in forty degrees-below weather. They had suffered from frostbite, neglect and most of all from malnutrition. Scores had died in the past few weeks because they had finally lost the will to live under the terrible conditions and especially the boring diet and the routine of uncertain discipline.

If we were scared before, the sight of these poor guys now frightened us even more. Would we be like that in a few weeks? In fact, we were all very thin but it was the look of desperation in their eyes and their slowness of movement that was most disturbing.

Our meals were collected in scoured baked-bean tins just before dark. They usually consisted of boiled sorghum, the consistency of stodgy rice and tasting like cardboard soaked in iodine, with either a half tin of haricot type beans or fried cucumber with some rock salt and sometimes Chinese cabbage boiled in water. There were two meals a day, one before dawn. If you were really sick you were allowed the crust from the side of the cooking bowl. However, we were young and famished so we wolfed it down in a very short time, scrounging from anyone who could not stomach the meal. After seven weeks on the march and two in a confined space of an underground dugout, we had soon learned that we could not expect to be fed on a regular basis, sometimes going up to three days without official feeding times and stealing anything at all edible and learning to eat it there for we were regularly searched for contraband and punished for possessing any stored foodstuffs. Two regular meals a day seemed a luxury even though monotonous and hard to retain in one's system for many minutes, especially the beans. We soon learned to chew each bean separately, for we were puzzled when the whole bean was passed so soon after the meal that it could not possibly be doing the body any good.

Later we were to witness many cases of men who just could not swallow another mouthful and simply decided to die. One young Kansas marine accomplished this within twenty-four hours of his decision. He was a fine-looking chap, unlike the zombies down the road. His six-feet plus body was as heavy as the four of us could carry on the stretcher. Fortunately some other guys scraped the hole for the shallow grave. As for us, we made group pacts to force each other to live, keep some kind of exercise going, and talk incessantly about tomorrow, what we would do and eat once we got out. We talked and slept from dawn to dusk, and huddled together for warmth. There were ten of us confined to an eight by four feet room, five aside, sleeping with our feet under each other's armpits, dirty, lousy, hungry, but despite everything hopeful that it would not be for very long. Certainly we would be home before next Christmas! We had to be, for if the situation did not change for the better we would all be dead and we certainly were *not* going to die, especially after all we had been through on that blasted march. Perhaps later the Chinese would recognize us as prisoners-of-war and give us Red Cross parcels?

Night falls fast in Korea. With the darkness the guards got jumpy about our frequent (up to twenty times a day) visits to the latrine, an area of wooden boards over pits where one squatted, one foot on each side.

Each Korean house had its complement of cockroaches which came out of the ceiling and the walls as soon as it was dark to feast on us. Some insects who were slow to move at first light were soon bloody smudges on the walls where they had been swatted by angry victims. Apart from the elementary accommodation and the lack of sanitation, one of the most degrading problems was trying to rid ourselves of marauding insects.

It was a severe shock to realize that our concern for each other could melt away rapidly. Soon bodies become just bodies if you do not know their names. There were just so many for the fatigue party who had to dig the holes, cursing their inconsideration in dying and thus becoming a heavy chore. When the early winter rains came the bodies were all washed out again, so we had to dig larger, deeper trenches and put some rocks on top. We felt that the War Commission could not possibly know who was who, or how many there were in all the trenches we dug. One held approximately thirty-seven, although we found two extra legs and one arm, but definitely thirty-seven skulls. There were ten such ditches dug over the next year.

By the spring of 1952 the Chinese Peoples' Volunteers had recognized that we were P.O.W.'s and had reported names of the survivors to the Korean truce talks. Our bodies adapted to somewhat better conditions. The boredom remained, however, and our hopes ebbed and flowed with the progress of the peace talks.

By August 1952 we had been P.O.W.'s in Chungsong, North Korea for over fourteen months. Our bodies and minds had adapted to the routine. The weather had been lovely for the past several weeks and American bombers had kept away from our area. All we had to do was wait for the peace talks to conclude, just hang in there. The Chinese had pretty well given up on the brainwashing; they had found out dialectic materialism was way over our heads.

So there I was feeling secure in the tight-knit group we had been forced into. In fact, I was playing basketball one day when a Chinese officer stopped the game and singled me out to follow him to the office. There I was handed over to two guards and marched out of the compound area, about five miles down the road to a large Korean house which appeared to be heavily garrisoned. No one spoke to me in English; they shut me in a room with no blankets or furniture, just a dirt floor, no windows, but with some light filtering through the bars high up on the door. I attempted to look out but was stopped by the guard with many angry wavings of rifle and bayonet. Apparently he considered me a highly dangerous foreign devil. I retired to the far end of the eight-feet square cell and became very lonely and apprehensive. There had been rumours of interrogation centres from which people seldom returned.

There appeared to be several other occupants in similar small rooms around the quadrangle, but any attempt to communicate was sure to infuriate the Chinese. Whatever I was there for it certainly was not a P.O.W. convention.

The walls were built of mud over a bamboo frame and I was pleased to discover a flaw in the mud about twelve inches above the floor through which I could gradually make out another Korean house, not forty feet away. A civilian family still lived there, a Mama-san, a Poppa-san, a very old man and several children. Their routine and evidently happy life in poverty-stricken conditions, were a small, crack-sized glimpse of another world ouside my cell.

We were allowed to go to the latrine once per day and most days were fed soon after. One learned to eat whatever mess was provided within five minutes, for once I had tried to save some for later in the day and the guard came and took it away despite my pleas. Washing and shaving facilities were non-existent and I had no comb. After the first night I was lousy again.

Eight weeks of solitary in these conditions took its toll on me mentally. I was feeling really sorry for myself, when one morning my Korean family next door seemed really excited. A young North Korean soldier had joined them and it was obvious that this must be the son of the house who had arrived home unexpectedly. Mama-san was crying and clinging to her son, and in fact things were just as they would be in our own world. And I wept too for the joy in the Korean home, and prayed to God that my own homecoming would be equally ecstatic.

Three days later I was returned to my comrades in the prison camp — and that too was like coming home. The security of trusted friends and being back in the herd put a wonderful complexion on the present and gave me renewed strength for the future. The fifty-seven days of solitary confinement proved to be the most uncertain, precarious, frightening and lonely time of my life.

Later it transpired that I had been punished for being argumentative over the communist doctrine, thus showing myself to be "an enemy of the Chinese people" and in fact I had to write several self-criticisms of my prior actions before being allowed back with my fellow prisoners.

By the end of July 1953 we had lacked news for several weeks on the progress of the peace talks. Then on July 27th, after the morning roll-call, we were marched to the central parade square at the far end of the compound. There we were ringed with many extra guards; heavy machine guns were also in evidence. We feared the worst.

The camp commandant started his usual speech in Chinese implying that Mao Tse Tung's hordes had given us leniency and the fact that we were still alive proved it. We continued to be unimpressed by his generosity. The interpreter at this point, looking rather embarrassed, informed us bored, disinterested lot that an agreement had been reached at the peace talks. We failed to react. Then we did a double-take. What had he said? Had we heard him right? Suddenly we were agog to hear what the poor man had to say next. Certainly he had never had such an attentive audience. The guards got fidgety; there was much clicking of rifle bolts. And still the commandant ranted on with waving arms. The tension was terrific we could not believe it, maybe he had got it all wrong. Then a smile came over the interpreter's face when he said the cease-fire would come into effect at ten a.m. that day.

There were a few cheers, but most guys were saying, let's hear the catch. Yes, he said, we would be going home soon if the agreement was not broken. Then everyone started talking at once; the guards got really agitated; apparently the commandant wanted to say some more, but no one was listening. Eventually some of the guards shot a volley over our heads just to get our attention. It worked all right. The commandant shouted loudly in Chinese, obviously addressing the guards and the camp leaders. Next, to our surprise, he said in English, "Good luck to you chaps and to you guys".

On August 16th, nineteen days later, I was among thirty-five British and American P.O.W.'s exchanged at Panmunjom after two years, three months and twenty-two days in Chinese custody. I was twenty-two years old and felt extremely lucky to be alive and going home.

11
1917

The Watson Family

Dear Miss Watson:

I very well remember meeting you at Cumberland In The Field January 12th, 1917 and am glad that you wrote to me in your trouble. I only wish that I were in a position to alleviate the terrible anxiety under which you are all suffering, but I cannot. I can only say that your brother is still "Missing", and there is a fair chance that he may be a prisoner. I dare not advise you however, to build too strongly on this possibility, as I think you would have received word from him in that event prior to the date of your letter.

The facts are these:- On the night of Nov. 10-11, my Battalion took a leading part in an attack on German trenches; perhaps you have heard of Regina Trench. On this occasion we captured the last portion of the trench then remaining in German hands.

Prior to the attack your brother with three others was on duty as an advanced post, acting both as observers and pickets; they had orders to return before midnight. They did not return; a party went out to bring them in, but could *find no trace of them. After the conclusion of the attack, when counter attacks had been repelled and the enemy's retaliatory bombardment ceased, a thorough search was conducted, but no trace could be found of any of them.*

I regret that my letter leaves you as ignorant of his exact fate as before. I wish I could write more comfortable words. I can only say that he may be a prisoner. In the other contingency — this means that the party was annihilated by a shell bursting in their midst. If this were the case you at least know that he knew no pain, but died instantaneously.

You may be proud of your brother. He was a soldier and a man, and whatever his exact fate, he met it at the post of duty.

Yours sincerely, J. W. Warden, Lt. Col.

Sam was indeed a prisoner.

After capture, the four Canadians were not kept together. Sam was imprisoned with British soldiers right behind the German lines and within range of Allied guns. These men were each given a paper entitled "Declaration to English Prisoners of Respite". The preamble stated that as Prisoners of Respite they would be kept "very short of food, bad lodging, no beds, hard work, no pay, no soap for washing or shaving, no bath, no towel or boots" and so on. The balance of the paper advised the prisoners to write to the English Government, describing their plight and suggesting that until Germans held in England were given better conditions this ill treatment would continue. Writing materials were offered.

In the first eleven months many men died of starvation, overwork and other causes. During this time they were imprisoned in nine different camps, old barns and similar places. For these eleven months there were no fires, no blankets, no showers or bath or toilets, no soap or change of clothes. Over Christmas 1916 there were five days without food. When there was food it consisted of a tin of soup made from dried vegetables, a quarter loaf of dark bread and coffee made from burned barley and chicory. They were made to work on roads, railroads and unloading barges.

From the fall of 1917 on there was an improvement, in that the prisoners were moved about fifteen miles back from the Front. Red Cross parcels began arriving and families could send letters and gifts. Sam's weight increased from the eighty-five pounds he had been reduced to.

By the middle of September, 1918 the Allies were advancing and in this section the Germans were pushed back to Mons. Then in October they and their prisoners were at Liege. With the Armistice the prisoners were freed and made their way to Calais where camps were established. Sam reached England on December 1st, 1918 and was returned to Canada the following April.

12

Shot Down Over France

Don Morrison

from a taped interview

It was 1942, and I was leading a flight of Spitfires. We were escorting some B17's to a bombing raid on a steel works. We had no problems; we seemed to have done a good job of the bombing. On the way back, as we were coming toward the French coast, I ran into oxygen problems. My system gave out. About the same time, German planes came up behind us. Being short of oxygen, which is almost like having a slight drunk, I turned back towards a German fighter. One of the fellows told me afterwards that he had seen myself and my wing man chasing two 190's and four more 190's were all in a line behind us. Eight of us in line together.

A very short time later my wing man was shot down, one of the 190's was shot down and so was I. My wing man — he was Doug Manley from Wetaskawin, Alberta — had his plane on fire. He had been about to land when, coming in over the French coast, he flew over anti-aircraft batteries and they nailed him. He had his wheels down and was obviously about to touch down. In addition to him, six or seven people in the house that the plane crashed into were killed. Doug is buried in a small cemetery in that part of France.

For myself, I was most fortunate. I was hit in the leg by a cannon shell which blew it off, and I left it in the airplane when I bailed out. I drifted down quite some distance. As I was close to coming down to land, German soldiers stood shooting at me with rifles. I guess they weren't good shots because none of them hit me. I landed in a small farmer's field across the canal from the Germans who, in the meantime, were shouting and pointing rifles at him. The farmer and another chap wrapped me in my parachute, laid me on a ladder, and took me in a small punt across the canal to the Germans. The Germans, when they saw me, realized the condition I was in, flagged down a truck and took me four or five miles to a Luftwaffe hospital in St. Omer. I was unconscious for ten days but I did survive and eventually found my way to Dulag Luft and Stalag III.

In the hospital, they operated on my leg and treated my other leg, which was fairly badly burnt. It was about two months later that I was able to leave and go to Dulag Luft. There they finally removed the cast. It was a rather peculiar treatment for burns. They had smeared the wound with whale grease and put a cast on it. I'd never heard of that before, neither had anyone else but it was successful because I haven't had any trouble with the leg since.

I was only a prisoner-of-war for a year, because I came home with the first repatriation of the badly wounded.

A few years ago I went back to St. Omer to try to find some of the people who had helped me — seen me go down, perhaps seen part of my airplane, or whatever. I wrote to the newspaper that covers that area of France and they published a story. I got several replies, some from people who had seen my airplane come down, some who had seen *me* come down, and one from the farmer who had picked me up and wrapped me in my parachute. I actually met him again! I also found out that when the Germans were standing and shooting at me, a lady who lived in the house did a great deal of shouting at the Germans to the point where she was taken away to a concentration camp. She returned from the camp but, unfortunately, died a year or so before I came back to France so I didn't have a chance to talk to her.

It was a strange feeling for me to go and look at my wing man's tombstone in the French cemetery and realize that he hadn't himself been hit, only his airplane. He should have got away with it. By the same token, I should never have gotten away with it.

13

Marseillaise

Antoine Masson

I was among the prisoners in a former French military training camp near Verneuil-sur-Leure.

There were nearly three thousand of us in the sprawling unsanitary camp. Many of us were wounded, many in rags, and living conditions were horrible.

I was one of one hundred and twenty-seven officers, and though we were kept apart from the enlisted men, we got the same food, which was little and poor.

The menu never varied: In the morning we were given a bowl of watery soup and a little bread; at noon bread and a small piece of inferior cheese; in the evening a cup of ersatz tea and some bread. In all we got about two hundred grams of bread a day.

After a few days we began to feel the effect of such a diet but we had no way to supplement it.

Red Cross parcels, which meant to prisoners-of-war the difference between barely existing and living well, had not begun to arrive.

Other conditions at Verneuil-sur-Leure were about on a par with the food. We were given inferior plastic spoons to eat with and they kept breaking into little pieces. You would attempt to get a mouthful of soup and end up with a mouthful of spoon as well.

On our twelfth day in that camp we were marched three miles to the station where a train was waiting to carry us to the prison-camps farther from the coast.

Our badly wounded were placed in trucks; the walking wounded were aided by their companions. We marched three abreast flanked by Nazi guards, including motor-cyclists who rushed up and down each side of our lines.

Our officers, headed by a Brigadier marched at the rear.

Our route took us through the town of Verneuil-sur-Leure. We were spread out into a long line. I imagine the Nazis stretched us as much as possible to impress the French people with the great numbers of prisoners.

The men started off orderly and silent, but they no sooner left the camp than someone in the front ranks began singing the *Marseillaise*. Another voice caught it up then another and still others, until the song swelled down the entire length of the line of march.

A lot of the English boys did not know the words, but they did not let that stop them, and added to the swelling volume of song.

It was the only time at Dieppe or after that I saw the Nazis get really excited. Their commanding officer rushed up to the Brigadier and said, "You make them stop or I can't control my men."

It was the Brigadier's turn to grin, "I am afraid," he said, "this is the one time I can't control mine."

By now we were in the middle of the town. Apart from turning machine guns on us there was nothing the Germans could do.

Frenchmen poured from their homes, and stood up on the porches and on the streets. Blinds shot up in the shop windows, and in nearly every one you could see a French woman, usually sobbing and holding up a child, but always looking proud and smiling.

At the corners men and boys of the village stood in groups. Our men would break off singing to call to them that, though we were prisoners, others would be coming. They called out that it would not be long, and everyone made the V sign and laughed and sang.

The French smiled and waved at us. Some of them signalled openly, others performed rather a neat trick. As we approached they would light a cigarette and hold it deep down between their fingers. It looked like the V sign, but how could the Germans prove it.

As we arrived at the station French Canadians and English Canadians were reaching out and patting each other and many officers were crying, not tears of beaten men but the expression of emotion of a very proud and happy group.

A lot of hard-boiled officers wept that day who had not wept since they were children.

On the train we were all a little sheepish, but nobody was ashamed. Many agreed we had uncovered one of few genuine secret weapons of this war. It was the *Marseillaise*.

14
Home Run Via Russia

Alex C. Masterton

from a taped interview

I was raised in Winnipeg until I was seventeen. Then my family returned to Scotland, where I attended the University of Edinburgh to study engineering. However, I dropped out to join the British territorial army in 1939. In January, 1940 I was sent to France with the Argyll and Sutherland Highlanders.

On arrival in France we were immediately dispatched to the Belgian border where we were set to digging fortifications. The Maginot Line hadn't been completed to the sea and so we were busy digging, under terrible conditions. It was an awful winter, the snow and ice were terrible. We were expected to dig fortifications from the Belgian frontier in these conditions — which we did.

In April, 1940 the Division was moved to the Maginot Line, where we were installed, not *in* the Maginot Line, but between the Maginot and the Siegfried Lines, in a sort of no-man's land. There we saw our first Germans and some action.

When the Germans broke through the Sedan on the 10th May, 1940 we were moved from the Maginot Line, brought to Paris and back onto the Somme. The Germans were at this time trying to surround Dunkirk. The 51st Division were near Abbeville, south of the German thrust to the sea. We fought the Germans there until the 8th of June, when it was decided that the 51st Division would be evacuated from France through Le Havre. We were in the process of marching on Le Havre in convoy when we ran into another arm of the German army that came through Rouen that morning and had reached the sea near a place called Fecamp, on the French coast. We ran smack into a German ambush. I was near the front of the convoy and we tried to put up a bit of a fight. At that particular time there were two destroyers going up the English Channel. I later found that one was called *H.M.S. Bulldog* and the other one *H.M.S. Boadicea*. They were obviously watching what was happening; they put in cutters and took a number of men off from the rear of the convoy, but we at the front were in a fire-fight with the Germans.

There was a fellow with a Bren gun ahead of me, and the chap that was loading for him was hit between the eyes. The Bren gunner motioned, would I come and load for him. I crawled forward and was loading the Bren when I saw out of the corner of my eye an object arching towards me. It turned out to be a German potato-masher, or hand grenade. It went off with a hell of a bang, but I just felt a thump on my leg and thought no more about it until the fight was over.

A German came forward and motioned for me to get up. I found that my leg was numb and I wasn't able to stand. I tried, but I fell down again. And then I realized that I had been wounded. My boot started to fill with blood, so I pointed to my leg. The German understood and I was allowed to lie there until a couple of our chaps picked me up and took me back to the German lines. The Germans had a lot of tanks and I was taken back into the tank lines and allowed to lie with a number of other wounded in a little school yard. The Germans had been decent enough to put down a little bit of straw for us.

I lay on the straw all night while six or seven of the badly-wounded died. We had no treatment. The next morning a German doctor came around and looked at the wounded, and identified those he thought should go to hospitals. We were taken to a hospital near Fecamp but found that the wards were full of German wounded. They allowed the French wounded to lie in the corridors, on stretchers, but the British were made to lie on stretchers on the lawn outside. We weren't able to get into the hospital. Someone had put my own field dressing on my leg.

About eleven o'clock in the morning a German doctor came around with an orderly and examined the various wounded people; there was a piece of shrapnel sticking out of my leg. I think it had jammed into the bone. He simply bent down and, with a pair of forceps, pulled the shrapnel out and poured about half a bottle of iodine into the raw wound, and that was it. Excruciatingly painful, but it must have worked because I was out of there within three days and on the march into Germany.

The march was terrible. We walked from near Fecamp into Holland. And the Germans were very, shall I say, inconsiderate. The water we drank was from the ditches. It was a very hot summer and we were made to march an average of forty kilometers a day on little food. Because of my recent injury, I was feeling a little shaky. That made no difference. We were made to march that forty kilometers per day.

A lot of us got dysentery because of drinking water from the ditches. It was July by now, and the wheat was getting high and ripe; we dashed into the wheat fields to relieve ourselves. A friend of mine from the Argylls dashed into a wheat field and fainted; when he came to the stars were out and there wasn't a soul around. He went to the first

farm house he came to. The farmer took him in. He worked on the farm until 1942.

In '42, he thought, "I'm getting nowhere here." He
went down to Paris; the farmer gave him a bike. He went
to Paris to try to contact the underground. The Gestapo stopped him, said he had stolen the bike and threw him into
a French jail. As soon as he got into the French jail the
French gendarmes knew right away that he wasn't French
so they said, "Who are you?" And he said, "I'm Belgique."
And they said, "No, you're not Belgique, tell us who you
are." And he said, "I'm a Scotchman." "Okay. Tell these
idiots that you've stolen the bike, they'll be happy and we'll
look after you." So he did. I think he got three months in
jail for stealing the bike. The French looked after him. He
was released from the jail and he went right back to the
farm where he had been. He had nowhere else to go. He
couldn't contact the underground. In 1944, the farmer called him and said, (his name was Jock, but the farmer called
him Jacques), "Jacques, come and see what's happening."
Apparently up the road were three American tanks; he stopped the first tank and he said, "I'm a Scotch soldier. I've
been here since 1940." The Americans said, "Bugger off,
we're too busy. Go on back. Just keep going back." So he
went back and he was finally sent home in 1944. He was
never captured but he never was able to escape from
France. . .

We were marched into Holland, and taken up to the
Rhine through the Zuider Zee in coal barges that hadn't
been cleaned out. Our fellow prisoners included a lot of
Moroccans and French Senagalese. At a place called Wessel
in Germany we were put on trains. It was a very hot summer and we were locked in the boxcars for three days and
three nights without food or water. We arrived in what we
later discovered was Poland. On that journey approximately
fifty people died, four in my boxcar.

We were taken to Thorn — now called Torun — the
birthplace of Nicholas Copernicus, the astronomer, where

we were housed in big tents, marquees, under the most primitive conditions. We were fed one bowl of watery soup a day; made from horse's heads. Every two days we had a fifth of a loaf of bread. People were dying quite regularly from starvation and lack of medical attention. There were two doctors in the camp, both of them British Lieutenant-Colonels, who had absolutely nothing to help us with. They had no medical supplies at all. The Germans didn't give them any.

We stayed there until the end of October when it gets very cold in Poland, much like the Prairies. It's a sort of continental climate; it's very cold and the winds from Sweden come roaring down across the Baltic Sea. It was obvious that if we weren't all going to die the Germans would have to move us. . .

There were about twenty-three hundred in the camp. We were moved in the beginning of November into what we called Fort 17. This was an old Polish fort that had been built in the area. Torun and Bromberg had been fought over many, many times and this was a Polish fort that was built mostly underground. Again the conditions were absolutely primitive. We suffered terribly. This is where the lice and the scabies first made themselves really manifest. We had lice almost from the time we were captured. The scabies were very bad and starvation was rampant.

There was no doctor in the camp, but a German doctor would come around once a week and I reported to him. My treatment for scabies was to be put under a cold tap, sort of a shower but no hot water, just cold, wash down, made to rub the scabs off my scabies (the scabs slide off very easily, and there's a slime underneath). Then we were made to smear ourselves (there was quite a number of us, at least twenty-five with the same condition), with a black sulphur ointment. Of course we didn't have any change of clothing. Here we were, made to cover ourselves in this black sulphur ointment, then we had to put our clothes back on, so we were consequently stuck to our underwear by the sulphur ointment. However, I must say, that it did have an effect. And it did seem to clean up the scabies condition, except the scars didn't go away for a long time. They persisted for at least a year.

After that I was moved to Fort 11, which was another fort in the area. In April '41, I made an attempt to escape. I climbed through the wire and onto a train, I got to within 150 kilometers of Berlin. I was told that the train was going to France but it didn't. It stopped; it was full of lumber and the lumber was being unloaded so I got off and started to walk. I had crude civilian clothes which really wouldn't have fooled anybody but I managed to stay free for five days.

I was captured because I had gone into a hayloft to sleep and had forgotten to take my boots under the hay when I took them off but left them on top of it. A woman coming in to feed the cattle in the morning found my boots and naturally figured there was someone under the hay. I was rousted out of there by a German forester. The Germans are great for uniforms, and everybody had a uniform from the postmaster to the foresters. He was armed and I thought he was going to shoot me, but he didn't. I was taken to Berlin, the police were called, and I was put in jail until the camp was notified. A guard came from the camp and picked me up. The Germans weren't unkind. The German police were all right. They were fine. I was a bit of an oddity, I suppose, in those days. I was taken back to the camp and given thirty days solitary for my attempt to escape.

Before I was sentenced I was taken to the local German headquarters. I was shown into a room; it had the two lightning strikes of the SS and on the door it said SS Sonderfuhrer Lampersbach. When I went in, Sonderfuhrer Lampersbach was sitting behind his desk, "Oh, come in, Masterton," he said, in perfect English. I sat down. He said, "You're Canadian." And I said, "Yes, sir." He said, "Well, so am I." I said, "You! What are you doing in the SS?"

"Well," he said, "that's another story." He said, "I was the manager of the Royal Bank of Canada in Weyburn, Saskatchewan for ten years before the war. My wife is from Vancouver. In 1938, I answered the call of the Fatherland, came back and, here I am, in the German SS." He paused, then said, "You're a Canadian and I'm a Canadian. If you'll just tell me where you got your maps and your civilian clothes, I'll see that you get a light sentence." I said, "Come on, you can't believe that I'm going to believe that with you sitting there in SS uniform."

So the two German guards came up and he said, "Take the swine away." That was the last I saw of Sonderfuhrer Lampersbach. When I got home I wrote to the Royal Bank of Canada in Weyburn, Saskatchewan. They never answered my letter. I think that's indicative of something. . .

Solitary confinement was boring. A completely different experience than anyone can imagine. I finally decided that if I was going to survive thirty days solitary I would have to devise a means of keeping my sanity. So I recited everything I could remember. I tried to think of the things I was going to do when I got out of the situation I was in. But it was awful. Solitary confinement is a cruel punishment. I didn't have any ants or mice or any friendly little things in my cell to cheer me up. The only little break I got was in the morning, when all those in solitary were made to come out and wash in a trough, and we managed to have a few words with each other. We were fed the same old soup and black bread. We weren't allowed any fat at all. At that time, we received a tablespoonful of lard per week and a tablespoonful of ersatz jam per week. But we were not given that in solitary.

Actually, I think the guards felt a bit sorry for us. I think that they felt it was rough treatment. Some of the Germans were quite interested in the fact that we had been front-line soldiers. Most of them hadn't been. The German was quite a soldier and he respected other soldiers, especially those who had been in action.

There were no Red Cross parcels in solitary. The first Red Cross parcel we received was in January '41, not long before I made my escape. There were twenty articles in the parcel and one parcel was shared among twenty men. We drew lots for the articles in the parcel and here I was starving, and you know what I won? — the bloody soap! So I traded it to a German guard for six cigarettes. I took a puff of the cigarette and passed out.

After I got out of solitary I was made to work (I was only a corporal) at a place called Bromberg; it's now called Bydgoszcz in Polish. Polish was forbidden in our area. There were signs everywhere, "Hier wird nur Deutsch gesprechen." I didn't learn Polish but I did learn German.

I worked for about two years in a sand quarry. In March, 1943 we had an altercation. The guard on our work gang, was an absolute madman. He shot one of our chaps, a fellow by the name of Feeney. Because I was the only one who could speak reasonably good German in the outfit, I went to the guard and I said, "Either finish poor Feeney off or get him some help or something." The guard became incensed at me, stuck a round in the breech, but the round jammed. He then took his rifle and went to smash his rifle butt into my face. I turned and got it in the back. I fell down and passed out.

When I came to, I was in the prison camp. At that time we had a doctor, who had been captured in Crete, a New Zealander, "I think they've broken your back," he said. I was urinating blood. But he said, "I don't know, without x-rays I can't do anything. I'm going to make you lie on this bed without a mattress." (We had straw mattresses.) "You are to keep perfectly still for as long as you possibly can." Well, that was the only treatment he was able to give me. And within three weeks to a month, I was able to get around. I have now a thirty-percent pension for my disability in the back.

In Bromberg, I was chained for eleven months. After the Dieppe raid. It applied to all the Canadians, even those serving in the British army. But it was really a laugh because we could get them off with a bully beef tin key. I was caught one day without my chains on. The kommandant said, "Where are your chains?" And I said to him, "Sir, can you believe that you're in this twentieth century, asking me, you who produced Goethe and Beethoven and Brahms and Schiller, you're asking me for my chains?" And he said, "I know, it's terrible, isn't it!" Well, anyway, I got reparations after that from the German government — fifty dollars for being chained for eleven months, from morning till night. They were decent enough to take them off at night. We had handcuffs and a chain running from our handcuffs down to the ankle chains. We could move around, we could hobble around, and it was fine with me — I didn't mind in the least. It was better than working the sand quarries. And I got fifty dollars reparations from the Germans and fifty dollars for being transferred by boxcar, which is against the Geneva Convention. So I got one hundred dollars in reparations from the West German government in 1949. In those days I was young and we were just starting to get a home together, and I wish I could have kept that cheque and framed it.

We had to cover four-storied concrete buildings with sand. We would load trucks and dump them, then lift the railway tracks up, dump, lift up, dump, lift up, and so on. The buildings were covered with sand and trees were planted on top. We later found that these were the buildings that were used to manufacture the explosives for the V-1 and V-2 buzz bombs. Because Peenemunde wasn't very far from us, where the rockets were being made by von Braun and Company. (Werner later became a good American.)

Before the manufacture of explosives, we were moved from there and I was sent to a farm camp in an area right on the Baltic coast where we dug peat. I got jaundice and was sent down to a prison-camp hospital in Danzig, or Gdansk, as it now is. There were two British M.O.'s in camp and by this time they had a fair amount of medical supplies sent by the Red Cross.

It was in Danzig that I first learned about the concentration camps, because one of our chaps had worked in one. His job had been to shovel the bodies of Jews into the oven. He had got some sort of infection from handling the cadavers, some sort of disease in his hands, and so he was brought into the prison-camp hospital. He said that in his estimation they had only put about seven thousand through the extermination process — I say *only* seven thousand to emphasize that was a smaller number compared to Auschwitz and Bergen-Belsen and the bigger concentration camps.

The chap was a British sergeant, in the Royal Scots. I'm amazed that the Germans allowed him to come back and tell his story among us. Our doctors were very interested in it. I do think, in retrospect, that these British doctors were in contact with Britain. They were particularly interested in what we could tell them about our camps. We were on the Baltic coast — had we seen any German submarines? and so on and so forth. The British, by this time, were very busy mining the Baltic with different types of mines, by aircraft of course. So they were very interested in the chap from the concentration camp. "Where were these people coming from?" They were asking questions; it was obvious, they weren't just asking for themselves. If they were in touch with Britain it would be a very closely-guarded secret as to exactly how. But by this time the Polish underground was forming. And they too were making contact with prisoners. So I would think it was probably through the Polish underground that these doctors managed to contact Britain.

After I got back to the peat-digging establishment, I was moved to a little camp with only ten Canadians and one guard. We were each made to work on an individual farm. Some of those farms in Germany weren't really farms at all, they were just little holdings. And each one went off

from the centre of the village, like the spokes of a wheel.
I worked for a woman who was a midwife. Frau Ber-
tram was a magnificent person who treated me like a son.
Her own son had lost a leg on the Eastern Front. Now he
was back at Gottingen University. Not long after I started
working there, he brought a fellow student who had been
a night-fighter pilot who had been shot down by one of
our bombers; he couldn't fly anymore, so he was allowed
to go back to university. We were all about the same age.
We had many fine discussions. Finally, we became so
friendly that I told them that I felt that I wanted to bog off,
and could they help me? They helped me because the war
was now being lost by the Germans. The Allies had landed in France by this time. They would help me if I would
remember them afterwards. This was agreed upon, and I
stuck to my bargain. After the war I was able to help them.
They supplied me with good maps, civilian clothes, a compass, and lots of bread before I took off. I was fortunate,
I was able to escape and get into the Russian lines.

This was how it happened: every night we were rounded up from the farm by the guard and locked into a little
room, not more than fifteen by fifteen in a brick building
that was surrounded by barbed wire. It had barred windows
and a heavy oak door. It was so well built and they had
such a good lock on the outside of it, we couldn't get it
opened. But we managed to get the bar out of the window
and go through it. We had a pair of pliers to cut the wire.
(The Germans were great for putting concertina wire on
the top, thinking we were always going to go over it. But
it was much easier to go through it.)

We naturally discussed our escape before we went.
There were eight of us in the camp, all Canadians. It was
a tiny camp with a guard who lived in the village inn; the
innkeeper was on the eastern front, so we all figured that
the guard was poking the innkeeper's wife, but we didn't
have proof of that. He was a bit of an idiotic type, a tailor
from Dresden, a humourless twit. He would come and let

us out in the morning and close us in at night. Usually we had to be back before dark, or as close after dark as we could. If we didn't, he would go out looking for us with his bicycle and his rifle.

We were discussing the escape one night, and Morris, a chap in the Service Corp who was the only son of a First World War widow, suddenly started to vomit and went to bed. And by God, in the morning, we woke up and he was stiff as a door-nail. He'd died in the night, and we don't know why, but he became very fat and we weren't having good rations at all. I think it was mostly edema, this fatness; his legs became swollen.

Rigor mortis had set in and we had a hell of a job getting his arms and legs in position to bury him. So we buried Morris, and then that left seven of us. Two decided they wouldn't go; they didn't want to risk it.

I collected the maps, compasses and other gear while the other chaps made their best effort to get some civilian clothes, but failed. I was the only one with fairly decent civilian clothes. So we abandoned that idea. We'd go in uniform, and to hell with it. The night we were to go, we worked on the bar on the window. Nobody had a watch; they were taken from us when we were captured. We estimated that it was about four o'clock in the morning when finally the bar came out of the concrete. Just as we were about to go through the window, we heard the squeal and roar of tanks. Here, by God, was a whole German tank battalion coming through the village, right in front of the camp. The road passed within twenty feet of the camp.

Well, we'd got the bar out, and were ready to go. Each of us was going to take a haversack, or a kit bag, with as much stuff as we could. We had great-coats; they had been sent by the Red Cross in about '43. By the time this damn German regiment passed by — the tanks took a hell of a long time — the guard banged on the door to tell us that it was time to get up. His method was that he would go back to the inn, have his breakfast, then open the prison door. He wouldn't even look at us, but would open the door, and we would wash in a sort of a trough. He'd allow us half an hour and by that time we were supposed to be ready for our farm. So we knew we had half an hour. It was almost daylight, by this time. We'd wasted the whole night getting the damn bar out and then the tanks came. So we went. And God, did we run! We ran and ran, and then we came to a road, a highway; we had to cross it. There was a whole German division going along it. Horse-drawn transport. We thought, well, we've got to cross it. There's only one thing to do and that's brazen it out. So we did. The Germans were so tired — they had been marching all night. They never even looked at us.

After we passed that highway, we split up, two and three. We three came to a big farm. It was a German farm, but we knew the area and knew there were Poles in it. I went into the stable where there was a Polish coachman and told him "Look, there's three of us and we're on the run. Can you help us?" "Yes," he said, "I can." He hid us in such a place that I'm sure he was in the Underground, because we went into the hayloft and down a ladder into a little box room that couldn't be seen from below. It had obviously been occupied by somebody else before us. We hid there for about three days until the hue and cry had calmed down.

We had to get to Torun, or Thorn, the old place that I had been in, because there's a bridge, the only bridge over the Vistula. The Vistula's a big river, and we had to get over it if we were going to get to the Russians. We finally got to a little Polish house just outside of the town. We tried it, and again we were lucky. The Pole didn't have anything to do with the Underground, but he was a railway man. We said: "We've got to get across the bridge." And he said, "The only way to get across that bridge is on a boxcar, because the foot traffic is checked by guards for passes."

We were lucky — we managed to get a boxcar, and

went across the bridge and it took us into Poland, about one hundred kilometers, right into eastern Poland. When we got off there, we went into a wood to hide. It was so cold and so still that night we could hear the rumble of guns. I didn't know that gunfire travelled such a long distance. It will travel a good one hundred and twenty miles on a still night. I didn't know; I thought we were within twenty miles of the Russkies.

Anyway, we finally got to a large house. Again the Poles helped us. They put us in the basement. The Poles told the owner that we were there. He was a German. His name was Baron von Baer. Luckily, he had two sons who had been captured by the Americans. They were writing back glowing letters of how well they were treated in prison camp. Von Baer came down to see us and said: "I'll feed you, I'll look after you, but if the Germans ever find you, I will know nothing about you." "Fair enough," I said, "fair enough." He said, "My wife and I are ready to go. As soon as we know that the Russians are within five miles of here, we're going." I said, "That's okay, that's great."

So we stayed in the cellar but we were warned that there were *feldpolizei* outside, that they would come around before anything fell into Russian hands — the scorched earth policy. The night before we met the Russians a bloody German artillery regiment took over the top of the house and we were in the basement. They didn't bother us, but we could hear them. Then suddenly at four o'clock in the morning, all the Germans took off. Great rush of trucks starting up and so on. Then about six o'clock we heard machine guns, so we knew we were at the sharp end by this time.

We were down in the cellar when we heard somebody come down. Jackboots have a particular sound and we'd been there long enough to know what they sounded like. We heard him opening doors; it was a big place, and the cellar had many rooms. In some, they had sauerkraut; in some, coal.

We heard him trying the doors, so we knew it was him or us. Racine, a chap in the Coldstreams, grabbed a big stick of kindling wood. We all stood at the side of the door, and sure enough when the door opened there was the bugger with his coal-scuttle helmet. Racine hit him right across the face with the piece of wood — but he didn't go down. By God, that guy died hard. It was a hell of a job to kill him.

We took off his helmet and we smashed him over the head with wood. He fought hard for his life, but we finally killed him. We took his Luger and pulled him down the corridor and stuffed him under the coal pile. Thank God, because shortly after that the fight got worse and the house was hit and caught fire, but we were safe enough because we were way down in the cellar. Then a tank came up. Of course, I couldn't see whether there was a star on it or a cross. Then one of the Poles who knew we were there came roaring down, bringing a Russian with him. The stupid Russian, shook hands with us and took off again, because he was fighting, you see. I went out to the tank, and was

Our Russian Allies

climbing up and shaking hands with the Russkies in the tank, when suddenly the Germans opened up and hit a tree beside me. A lump of tree came down and hit me on the head. The Russians waved me to go back to the house.

It was pretty dangerous out there, so I ran back to the house. There was a huge stained glass window, and just as I ran past it, a shell landed and blew the whole window on top of me. But I just kept on running and got down in the cellar when suddenly the fighting died down. We heard voices outside this little cellar window. We looked up, and here's three Russkies, with their bloody sub-machine guns pointed at us. "Come out of there," they said. They weren't the least bit friendly. They made us put our hands up and searched us, and found our prison tags that were in German, and the dumb buggers thought we were Germans, because it's written in German: "*kriegsgefangener*". Finally, they found the Luger that we'd taken from this *feldpolizei* type and this convinced them we were Germans. I couldn't speak but a couple of words of Russian. Finally, we were able to get them to come back down in the cellar and we spread the coal apart, and here's the chap that we'd done in under the coal pile. So then they understood where we got the Luger. We didn't want the damn Luger anyway.

We were taken back to Russian headquarters. I met Marshall Rokosovsky, of the Sixth Ukrainian Army and that was a disaster. He couldn't speak English and I couldn't speak Russian — I asked him if he could speak German. *Nyet.* So they brought along a German-speaking Russian and he began questioning us. I was made to sing "God save the King". With my voice, it's a wonder that they didn't shoot us.

We went back to Russia and it took us about five months to get out. It was a bad experience. Hunger again. I got onto an American ship in Odessa, but was taken off by the NKVD and sent back to a jail.

Then a British ship came in and took us to Istanbul. Turkey was neutral, at that time; they didn't come into the war until shortly before the end. We were met by the British Consul in Istanbul. He had civilian clothes for us, and we stayed there for three weeks. We were taken from Istanbul to Italy by a British ship that had come for fresh water. From Italy we got a troop ship back to England, almost three months before the war ended.

The two chaps on the final escape with me, after we had decided to split up, were Eugene Racine and a chap by the name of William Dick, from Prince Edward Island. I've never seen them since. No correspondence, nothing. After all we'd been through it seems a strange way to end a war.

15

"Good God, A Jew!"

Norman Rubenstein

It was my third escape. My companion and I had jumped a train near Prague. We were betrayed by a Slovak, who handed us over to a screaming Luftwaffe officer accompanied by a Dobermann.

"Murderers!" the officer shouted at us. "Terrorists and murderers! I should shoot you now!" He levelled the pistol in his hand at Len and then at me, and back again. The dog snarled and bared its teeth. It was a very tense situation.

I felt that this angry Luftwaffe officer may have lost family in a raid by British planes, which accounted for his rage at the sight of RAF uniforms. Certainly the reputation the Allied airmen had acquired was not one to parade before those on the receiving end of it — especially when the receiver was holding a gun at your head.

I told him in German that we had been prisoners of war for five years. He continued to fuss and fume and threaten, but gradually calmed down.

"You will be handed over to the police," he said. "They will know what to do with you. It is out of my hands."

The officer ordered us to walk with him to his house

where his manner changed completely. We spent most of that afternoon talking about the war and what the outcome would be. A Czech who worked with him told us that the peasant who had informed on us did so because he was afraid of the Russians.

We were taken from the Luftwaffe officer's house late that afternoon and, after a short train journey, handed over to the Czech Civil Police at a small police station in the Prague railway station.

The police were very polite and treated us kindly. "But we will have to hand you over to the SS," the officer in charge said. "The place they take you to — Theresientstadt — is not a very good place."

We spent the night in a cell in the police station and next morning two SS men came for us. I had not felt such fear and dread, mixed with hatred, for many years. I suddenly realized that for a long time I had felt a sense of adventure, a challenge, in making war against the Germans. These men, the SS, represented the very scourge of mankind to me. I would cheerfully have blown the building up and all of us in it to rid the earth of such scum. But I was not in charge here, not even of my own life.

Waiting outside the police station was a large truck, in the back of which were many civilians, and five SS men with machine guns. Len and I were roughly shoved and prodded up into the truck. It was March 23rd, 1945 — my day of infamy.

After we were aboard, one of the SS men came up to me and slapped my face. He turned to another SS trooper: "Good God, a Jew! I thought all the Jews in Europe had been killed long ago!"

It was not an encouraging start to the day. Again it convinced me that Germans who said they did not know what was happening to the Jews during the war, and continue to maintain even today they were ignorant of the atrocities, were and are lying — there is no other explanation.

We were driven a long way out of Prague, during

Sam and Phoebe Rubenstein, parents of the author, are shown here with two officials of the International Red Cross. The Rubensteins worked behind the scenes to aid POWs in Europe.

which time Len and I discussed what our eventual destination might be. He was optimistic. "It is probably a Straf (punishment) camp. I don't think we'll be there more than a couple of days." I was not so sanguine. I felt the Czech police were right when they said it was not a very good place.

This was confirmed when we finally arrived at what looked like a fortress similar to Fort Rauch, but even more sinister. It was located in an area of the town which was walled off and I assumed must be a ghetto. The gates of the fort opened and the truck with its load of human baggage continued into an even more securely enclosed section. The truck stopped.

As we were getting off, one of the SS men singled me out for a special shove so that I fell to the ground. "Here's a Jewish terror bomber murderer!" he yelled to other SS guards who were pushing and prodding the civilians off the truck and towards a building in the enclosure. As I lay on the pavement, my belongings were thrown on top of me.

"Get up!" the guard shouted, aiming a kick at me. I was feeling my back to see if I had broken anything, but I did not seem to be hurt. "Line up over here and stand at attention!" an SS officer shouted at the milling throng. A particularly sinister-looking man, heavily-built with dark hair and steel-rimmed glasses approached us.

"I am the Kommandant here," he said in German. "This is Theresienstadt concentration camp. You will work here. There is no way out — and you won't be going anywhere."

I had not heard of this camp before. Auschwitz, Treblinka, Belsen and the other horror camps were always in the news on the radio and in newspapers from everywhere but Germany. Why had we not heard of Theresienstadt?

The Kommandant went on to say: "My name is Jockel." A thin, tall, strong man with a cruel face stepped forward as Jockel said: "And this is my second-in-command, Rojko." The first thing Rojko did was to pull me out of the line. He slapped my face with both hands.

"What's in your kit, Jew?" he said. "Open it up!" I spread open my kit which contained my precious second pair of boots. They were beautifully shiny. Jockel looked at the boots and then at me. "You are a typical Jew!" he screamed. "Europe is starving and you have two pair of boots!" His jackboot went crashing into my spine. I staggered but did not fall. "We'll show you what boots are for!"

He and Rojko then pushed me against a wall and proceeded to kick me at the base of the spine while alternately giving me rabbit punches to the neck. Each time they punched my neck my forehead hit the wall. As my body bounced back, they both kicked me.

The beating went on for a long time until I was groggy and almost passed out, but I refused to fall to the ground where, I'm sure, I would have received an even more severe kicking from their heavy boots.

After what seemed an eternity, Jockel and Rojko stopped hitting and kicking me and swaggered back to the front of the lineup, laughing to themselves. "You are now going to get your haircut and have a nice bath!" we were told. A barber cut our hair to the scalp. At the baths, or showers as they actually were, we were ordered to strip. Our clothing was taken away. Other belongings were stacked in an outside room. My prized boots were gone, however, and I never saw them again.

I had left a bar of soap in my RAF jacket and did not feel like running out of the shower area and asking the SS to find it in the pocket. I don't know why I put the soap in that pocket in the first place and Len was annoyed with me. "Why did you do that?" he said. "Now we have no soap." We had to share soap with another British soldier.

It never occurred to us when we marched blithely into the showers that they might have been the sort that dispenses gas instead of water, a method that had been used to kill millions of Jews. They too had gone to their deaths — most of them — not knowing that deadly fumes would soon greet them. I learned later that gas chambers were being installed at Theresienstadt — or Terezien, as the Czechs call it.

Len became very apologetic about the soap incident. He was mad with worry about what was going to happen to me. So was I. "I have brought you so much trouble," he said. "I really am sorry." "That's not true," I countered. "I have made all my own decisions. You didn't force me to come along. Besides, I still don't think I am going to end up as a statistic. I'll survive and I'll see that you get back to England. Let's hope we both make it."

I knew deep down, however, that this was the worst mess I had ever gotten myself into.

Our clothes were returned from the "de-lousing oven". My jacket had an extremely antiseptic smell from the soap. Only a sliver of it had not dissolved.

We were again lined up after we had put our clothing back on. We were a strange-looking lot; men and women with hair cut to the scalp. Clothing hung on skeletons. Baleful looks from the SS; fear and trepidation from the skeletons.

I noticed a good-looking SS private talking to Jockel and Rojko who kept shaking their heads. Rojko came over to me and slapped my face. "Come, Jew," he said. As I stepped forward he called out: "Where is the other Jew?" A tall, thin man about thirty or thirty-five was shoved forward from a group who were watching us.

Three guards pushed the tall man and me to a big door in the surrounding wall. I was holding onto my belongings. The door opened into a room with two rows of cells. We were taken to a cell about halfway down the passage on the righthand side.

"Get in there!" the SS guards said, then shut a door behind us. I looked around at my new quarters. I had lived in some poor lodgings in my life, but these were the worst. The cell was empty except for a toilet which had no seat and no flushing system. The cell was less than four feet nine inches across (because I could not lie full length across it) and ten feet, less the toilet, in length.

It was painted a blinding white. One window made of wired, frosted glass was set deep in the rear wall. It was behind some bars and recessed so you could not reach it. Light filtered through but it was impossible to see out. The door, which had clanged shut behind us, had a peep-hole in it. As I was studying the meagre surroundings and meditating on how long we would be forced to remain here, the sound of a shot echoed down the chamber. Another shot followed it.

"What was that? Someone shooting?" I said. My companion, who seemed to know his way around the camp, said: "That's to make your friends think they have shot us. Don't worry yet. My name is Max Kobolovich. I come from Nathaniya in Palestine. Who are you?" I told him I was

Norman Rubenstein from Wales, a Lance-Bombardier in the British Army, Searchlight Unit.

"What are you doing here?" he said. "This is a terrible place." I freely admitted that I was more afraid than I had ever been in my five years of imprisonment. Yet I could not believe that I had come so far just to be killed in a concentration camp. After all that, this simply could not happen to me.

Max said our only hope lay with the SS private we had seen arguing with Jockel and Rojko. Apparently his sister had been interned for nearly five years in Britain and had received very fine treatment there. He was known to have saved many British lives.

"How long do you think they will keep us in here?" I said. "Maybe just one night," he replied. "I spent one night beforehand in a cell like this and then I was let out. So maybe we stay only one night."

Max told me that Theresienstadt, bad as it was, was the concentration camp where Jews hoped they would be sent to. "There is a chance here, even if you are a civilian and Jewish, a chance to survive." I wondered what the survival rate was when I was told that one hundred and forty-five thousand people had been killed or had died there in its six years' existence.

I thought about this for a moment. "If there are no gas chambers here, those must be individual murders," I said. "That's right," Max said. "Individual murders. These SS men like to kill that way."

It was then about mid-day and some food was brought in. To call it food is to honour it more than it deserved. It was a grey liquid which was called "soup". Wallpaper paste would have tasted better and looked more attractive. Max suggested we keep one-half bowl in order to have some liquid with which to flush the toilet.

About six that evening, more wallpaper paste was served, with some ersatz bread which Max said was mainly composed of sugar-beet peel.

Max, who had managed to hang on to his wristwatch, looked at it. "They count us at eight p.m. You have to stand at attention when they will probably kick and punch you again." I was not looking forward to this performance. With nearly two hours to spare, I opened one of the last containers of Red Cross food and shared it with my companion.

Just before eight p.m. there was a terrible noise as a man was dragged along the passageway screaming and groaning. He was thrown into the cell next to us. The guard quickly counted us and left. The man next door had been so severely beaten that we heard him scream for the next eight hours as he died by inches. "*Nie mehr hauen. Nie mehr hauen.* Don't beat me anymore."

The concrete-block walls between our cell and his were very thick, yet we heard him screaming in agony until four a.m. Gradually his voice weakened until he gave one final scream as he died. It had taken eight hours for him to die as a result of the beating the SS had given him. We slept very little that night. I was scared stiff and fearful of what the morning would bring.

By Max's watch it was close to seven o'clock when a guard and a civilian prisoner came around with "breakfast". They dished out some *ersatz* coffee. The guard looked at us and said, "The man next door died of a heart attack last night. Did you hear him? We sent a telegram to his family telling them what happened." We said nothing. I was too furious and sick to my stomach to trust my voice.

The civilian, who had a terrible grey, washed-out appearance, attempted to get into the guard's favour by saying: "Isn't it against the rules to have two people in a cell together? After all, they might indulge in sex."

I could not imagine anything less palatable than sex, especially with someone of the same gender, in a cell that was used to kill people in. I gave the man my most withering look.

There was no way of washing or shaving. This would

be the first time in years, other than on train journeys, that I had not shaved. If I was going to my death today, I still wanted to feel clean.

At eight-thirty a.m. the door to the cell was thrown open and the SS private, "our only hope", came in. In German he said, "Come. You are going to go on parade with your comrades. Then you will join your comrades in their big barracks. You will be treated from now on as military personnel."

I was so relieved I could have embraced him. Maybe it was only a respite, but it was a welcome change. I tried to thank him for what he was doing for us and asked him his name. He shrugged his shoulders. "Don't bother about that. Just keep out of trouble until you get out of here." He gave Max a significant look. Apparently Max had a way of getting into trouble quite often.

We went on parade and were quickly counted. There was no hope of escape from this fortress. Anyone who was not counted probably was too sick to stand or already dead. They then ushered us into a room which quickly became crowded. Two flush toilets were available to serve about six hundred of us. Almost every nationality was represented: Belgian, Russian, Yugoslavian, French, Australian, New Zealand, British, Canadian. The face I most wanted to see soon came smiling up to me through the crowd.

"Are you okay, Norman?" Len said. "God, I thought they shot you immediately after you were taken away. What a relief. Come over here. I've made some friends." I joined his group, among them some French and a Belgian. They all briefed me on our predicament. I was advised to go out only once or twice a day for some fresh air as they felt that I should be seen as little as possible. They warned me the guards killed on the slightest excuse. Max, my friend of the cell, was liable to bring on trouble at any time.

I looked around for Max. He was busying himself with some friends at another part of the room so I settled myself in as best as possible. I got some water and had a shave, then found a spare bit of floor and went to sleep on it.

When I woke up, Len was sitting by me, grinning with delight. Next to him was young Bill Harry, another POW who seemed always to be turning up in my life. "Oh, God, Norman," he said, "You are the last person on earth I wanted to see here. This is hell for Jewish people. When I saw you arrive yesterday, I really never expected you to be alive today. It's so good to talk to you now. But you've got to lie low."

Len said he was worried about me when he heard the two shots but he was immediately told by other British POWs that this was one of the SS "games" to make your friends think they had shot you. "Nevertheless, I was still very upset and worried until I saw you show up here today."

Bill Harry went on to explain how sometimes Jews were sent out to work by the senior inmate, called "the Kapo" in concentration camp lingo. One day one of the civilians, a Jewish man, had not done the work quickly enough to satisfy the SS guards. All the workers were forced to stand by and watch two guards as they knocked him down and killed him by cutting him and beating him about the head and body with two spades.

He described how the man had futilely tried to shield his head with his hands, only to have them smashed too. The murder took about ten minutes. The body was taken away and dumped in a mass grave.

I knew that if I got out of Theresienstadt alive, I would be a very lucky man.

I met and mingled with Russian prisoners more closely than at any other time. In some cases, more closely than I could have wished. The Russians occupied one of the toilets for sleeping quarters so if you had to use the facilities at night, you had a long wait. The walk to and from the toilet was over sleeping bodies. More often than not you stepped on someone's hand, arm or leg and were cursed for a fool. To add to this misery, you sometimes found it very difficult to find your sleeping place again.

The sleeping place consisted of a spot about the width of a twelve inch plank. To reserve the spot, you got your next door neighbour to lie on his back rather than his side, thereby saving some room for you when you returned.

On the second day at Theresienstadt, I noticed a Russian who had no shirt or jacket, bare from the trousers up. He must have suffered terribly from the cold, particularly at night. I offered him a woollen waistcoat my parents had sent me a year before and he was pathetically grateful.

Although Rojko had appropriated my pipe tobacco when I arrived, I found some comfort by keeping the pipe in my mouth as I strolled around the camp. To my great surprise, I was approached by my Russian friend bearing a small packet of tobacco, which he gave to me. It was every bit of tobacco he and his friends could find, including the dust in their pockets. He told me he and his comrades were so grateful for what I had done in giving him the coat.

However, when he asked if he could borrow my razor, I had to refuse. I always made it a rule never to loan my razor because so many men had terrible sores on their faces, I was afraid of catching something. I explained this to him and he smiled understandingly.

One of the Russians was in great pain; he had eight bullets in his left knee and couldn't walk. The Nazis did nothing for him and it was obvious that gangrene would soon set in. It was terrible watching him die like that. I did what I could by washing the wound, but surgery above the knee was what was needed.

I had been in the camp long enough now to begin to know my way around. Where I had spent the first night was in the punishment cells; next to them were the sick quarters. We were in a mainly Jewish block known as the "Kleinefestung" or "small fortress." If you were sick, as a civilian, you were sent to the sick quarters where ten or eleven people crowded into each cell.

Each man was given "sick men's rations", that is, one

ration of bread every three days and soup every second day "until you recover". When a man died, the others in the cell lay on top of his body so they could still obtain his rations. This went on until the corpse smelled so much it had to be given up.

During the time I was at Theresienstadt I counted thirty-three bodies carted out from the sick cells — men who had died from illness and starvation. One man in particular remains in my mind. He had startlingly black hair. This contrasted with the size of the rest of his body, the head seeming so large compared with the wasted remnants of his torso and abdomen. I was surprised to see how large the head appears when one has died of starvation. I realised that this was because the skull has very little flesh on it, being mostly bone. The rest of one's body appears to shrivel up — even the skeleton seems to become smaller.

Whenever one of these fleshless corpses were being carried out of the camp, a grim-humoured group of British soldiers exhibited their ghoulish sense of humour by remarking: "He's so thin, he won't even be worth putting in the soup." The rest of us could have killed them.

Most of my days were spent playing gin rummy with a Belgian, who somehow escaped getting his hair cut off. Other days I played with some French soldiers or went out once or twice a day for a walk around the square. We were not supposed to talk to people from other barracks or cells. However, one day I was called over by a young Norwegian who was sweeping the ground. He asked if I had heard that Roosevelt was dead. Apparently the Germans were announcing that "the world's biggest war criminal has died."

I could give him no definite word on that but when he asked about whether any of Norway was liberated I told him only Kirkenes near the Russian border. The Allies did not wish to make Norway a battlefield, I said. He was disappointed but I assured him that the war would soon be over.

As you may have noted, there was very little in the way of entertainment but we were soon to learn that *we* were to become the entertainment. One day we were all made to go outside while the SS men made two prisoners walk up and down the parade ground naked. On a wall above were some SS officers and their women, Brunhildas all — perfect Aryans, blonde or platinum blondes and very well-developed. They had a particularly hard way of turning to their SS men friends and laughing whenever they saw something cruel happening to the poor unfortunates below.

The entertainment was to whip these naked men with willow boughs until their lifeless grey-brown skin bled from many wounds. The excuse was that the men were lousy and this was one way to beat the lice off.

The big, blue-eyed blondes on the fortress wall would screech with laughter until it was decided that the lice had been beaten off for the day, then they would retire to their quarters with their SS officer friends.

These "ladies and gentlemen" would then come out and watch us parade and fight for our food each day. They found the whole exercise most amusing. I heard one woman say: "They are all animals! Very soon the Fuhrer will bring out a secret weapon and all the Allies will be defeated."

One day as they strutted around on the wall as though Germany had already won the war, instead of being within a short time of losing it entirely, I stood looking up at them, Len at my side. They were proud, arrogant and absolutely merciless. "You know, Len," I said. "I always say the German men are square-headed, but have you noticed that their women are square-titted?" Len looked at me for a moment before bursting out laughing. "Norman, I never thought I'd laugh in this hell hole, but that is a lovely remark."

For further entertainment, the guards would pick on the civilians, one game being to walk up to a man with a hat on and knock it off. He would be told to pick it up. If he kept his eyes on the guard and felt around for his hat as he bent down, meanwhile gently directed by his comrades, he was safe from a beating. But if he took his eyes off the guard even for a second, the guard shot him in the head. I couldn't keep count of the number of men I saw shot and killed this way.

On the seventh day I was talking to a Canadian we had discovered in this hell. We were talking together when three SS bullies dragged a civilian from a cell and struck him down with his rifle butt. All three then proceeded to smash their rifle butts down on the man's head until they appeared to have fractured his skull.

Suddenly they laughed, told the man to get up, which he barely managed to do, and called some of his cellmates to take him away.

The Canadian soldier, a fine, fair-haired young man, whom I met later in a pub in Hampstead, London, after the war, looked at me in consternation. "Oh, my God!" he said. "How can such things happen? I wonder if we will live through this?"

I replied that we had to live through it, to let the world know what went on. It just seemed that if the SS wanted some "fun" they would pick on any civilian and do what they liked with him or her. We had heard that only recently Jockel had knocked down a pregnant Jewish woman and had kicked and beaten her stomach until her child was aborted in terrible agony for her.

Our English captain told me on no account ever to let the Germans get my uniform. Once you were in civilian clothes you lost whatever protection you may have had as a soldier, leaving yourself wide open for brutalities such as just described.

One day our toilets were blocked and we were permitted to cross the parade ground to use the toilets in the Jewish civilians cells. The moment I entered, some of these prisoners, still in their suits from civilian life, came up to me and said: "You are English, and Jewish? Come, we must show you this."

They showed me their cells; four or five of them shared each one. In most of them the walls had been newly whitewashed, yet marks of blood as high as one's waist were beginning to come through the whitewash. Apparently the SS had been on a rampage some weeks before and had beaten many Jews to death, one at a time, in these cells.

"You must tell the world when you get out of here. The world must know what's happening. We may not live to tell about it. You must tell the world." With these instructions ringing in my ears, I tried my best to comfort them, promising to do what they asked, then stumbling outside to the relative peace and comfort of the other side of the fortress.

After more than ten days, a crowd of Czech civilians were brought in, aged from sixteen to eighty. One man in particular I remember who was well over seventy had lovely, long flowing white hair. The man's crowning glory was clipped off roughly by an SS man and I couldn't help thinking: "Poor chap. His hair may never grow that long again, even if he survives this place."

Surprisingly, on the twelfth day of our confinement we were suddenly told to get ready to leave! Nothing could seem so wonderful. One moment we seemed to be in hell — and almost miraculously, we were being taken out. The transition went swiftly, except for the wounded Russian who had to be carried out. We passed the ghetto where I was able to look over the wall and through a hole saw a dear old Jewish man hobbling along with a stick. I can still see him in my mind's eye today and only pray he survived.

Outside Theresienstadt we boarded cattle trucks, eighty of us to a truck, separated by nationalities, and moved off. The conditions were appalling, but it was better than other inmates of concentration camps were experiencing. There was no food, water or stops for sanitation for anyone.

The next morning we stopped and a few English, including Len and I, were marched off. We were told the wounded Russian had died that night in the Russian cattle-truck, obviously from gangrene.

Where we stopped was in a small Sudeten village called Asch. From this point where we disembarked, we were marched to a brick factory where there were some British and American prisoners under the control of an American officer.

We had scarcely found a place for our kit and bed before I heard a voice saying, "Good God, Norman! Is that you? Whatever happened to you? You look awful! Who's your friend? I'd better get you a decent meal!"

It was "1014" Jones, an old pal. No one could have been a more welcome sight.

16

Naval Prisoner

Hector H. Cooper

One could sense the tension mounting in those early days of 1944, as the invasion of continental Europe was becoming more and more inevitable. *HMCS Athabaskan*, a Canadian Tribal class destroyer, worked unceasingly on the task of clearing shipping lanes and dispersing enemy coastal convoys. It was a case of patrol all night and back in to provision all day, to be ready to proceed again once night fell.

The early morning hours had crept around on Saturday, April 29th. We were in company with our sister ship *Haida*. Enemy destroyers and 'E' boats were dead ahead. There were but the two of us. We knew we were outnumbered. The air seemed to stand still. The men were ready, waiting and listening, all set to leap into action at the order "rapid salvoes". And then it came — one salvo, two salvoes, and the ship shuddered, for we had taken a nasty one in the stern quarter. Director fire circuits were broken. Guns had to switch to local firing, but it was too late, because there was only one turret left in working condition. We were a sitting duck without heavy armament of defence.

"Prepare to abandon ship," was the order passed down from the bridge. Within minutes, a second enemy torpedo found its mark in the starboard side of No. 1 boiler-room, to end the ship's fighting career.

There was a sharp list to port, and the ship was settling fast. A scramble of bodies jumped, slid, and dived into the cold water below, followed by the swish of swimmers' arms and legs, labouring to get away from the once proud and sleek fortress of steel.

As the last trace of the forecastle slid from view, a few of us made rendezvous to a spot where we could see carley-floats. There we just waited in the wee hours and strove to keep afloat.

Some swimmers were picked up by our sister ship *Haida,* which had returned after routing the enemy convoy single-handed. Dawn was breaking, which prevented a long stay in any one spot, so *Haida* had to make a hasty retreat out of the range of the enemy shore batteries. After about five or six hours in the water, I was picked up by a German Albion class destroyer and was later taken to Brest on the French coast. It was frightening en route to undergo an attack on the ship by our own airforce. But we did arrive safely, shaken but intact, and as naked as the day we were born. Our clothing was badly oil-soaked and had to be discarded on boarding the German ship.

Once in Brest we were loaded on trucks and taken to a nearby convent for billeting. We were kitted out in discarded naval clothing, sufficient to cover one's body and to keep out the cold. Comforts in general were conspicuous by their absence. For five days we remained there, answering or refusing to answer questions thrown at us from right, left, and centre. This was our first encounter with the front line German and where we first experienced that once-boasted iron fist of German might, though by now, in 1944, in a somewhat crumbling state. We were massed together, some eighty strong, and rationed one bowl of soup each, three slices of sour bread and two cups of *ersatz* tea. We were not allowed to converse with one another. Numerous armed guards were constantly present to see that this rule was carried out. We were never allowed to become comfortable in any way, to the noticeable enjoyment of our Jerry guards.

On May 4th, we were trucked to the Brest railway station to begin what turned out to be a week of miserable travel. We were packed ten into a compartment meant normally for six, and locked in throughout the entire trip. We were still forced to live on the same meagre rations, but we did get an extra, an issue of three bitter French cigarettes per man. The train made two stops per day for latrine purposes, under strict guard. This wearisome journey, with the prisoners cramped into small quarters, with no place to rest our heads or stretch our legs, and with the train making slow detours around bombed railway sections, lasted through village after village and town after town. We never knew how long it would go on. Finally, we arrived, late one night, at our destination, a small village lost among the north-east German marshes.

It was a relief to stretch our legs again and, as we scrambled out and were checked into waiting vehicles, we all started to feel better.

Alas, when we arrived at the camp, we all found ourselves placed in solitary confinement.

The cell was cold and damp with one small window for light and air. The severest of punishment awaited anyone who violated the rule that occupants must not look out of the window, which was just above eye level. Food became desperately scarce. There was no reading. Sanitary conditions were lacking — a single latrine for the whole block. There were no smokes, except when an interrogator was present. A hard straw mattress and a jute pillow served as a bed on hard boards.

The days grew long, while the interrogations continued

relentlessly. I could feel my body and soul sinking and my strength diminishing. I chewed straw from my pillow to ease the pangs of hunger. I just sat or paced the short floor for hours at a time, to conserve sanity, always thinking of home, thinking of the past, wondering if I was as lucky as I had thought I was to be alive. Still, here I was and I must grin and bear it, come through somehow, for so much awaited me back home if I could survive. Thoughts of my wife and infant son were all I had to ease the loneliness.

One June day I was told to get ready to go to Camp Dulag. I had lost count of the days and weeks of solitude, but I was able to calculate later that it was about thirty-eight days that I spent in solitary confinement. I welcomed the prospect of seeing my shipmates again. When the guard came, in my eagerness to get going, I didn't realize how much my legs had weakened, for they buckled under by the third step outside. Two guards then half carried me between them to Dulag, a short distance away. It was great to be placed among my fellow prisoners-of-war once more. A Red Cross food parcel was issued to me. I began eating and eating until I became violently sick. I was later to learn that my normal weight of one hundred and eighty pounds was now one hundred and twenty-eight. However, for the next three weeks that I remained in Dulag, I began feeling somewhat stronger.

We were then moved to Marlag M, a cosmopolitan camp of marine types of all nations. At least here, if health permitted, one could partake of sports or go on decent walks within the larger compound. We were now left much more to ourselves, and other than three daily *appels*, or check-parades, daily routines were dull.

Facilities were still poor and one had to makeshift for oneself. Food and clothing were scarce and, as time went on, the Red Cross parcels, intended to be weekly, diminished first to every two weeks and then to one a month, by Christmas 1944. We had to improvise means of cooking by making up miniature forges that would force-burn the

Cooking on Blowers

tar out of the road pavement. Small potatoes and field tur-
nips were the mainstay when we could obtain them through
barter or the outright robbing of gardens.

Water, not plentiful, was hauled in by hand in tub-
wagons. Dishes were often cleaned by using dry sand. You
learned to be resourceful and to prepare meals in as many
different ways as possible.

I had the misfortune to contact a mouth disease that
bared all the roots of my teeth. With the help of a German
military doctor, I was treated with a black medicinal powder
held adjacent to the roots of my teeth by a form of mud-
pack. Over a three-week period, I could only take in liquids
through a plastic straw. When they removed this plaque
from my mouth, the deterioration appeared to be stopped,
but my gums were tender and sore for most of my camp
stay. By spring of 1945, I had regained about twenty
pounds. of my lost weight, but still could not exert myself
in any of the normal sporting activities of the camp.

With the breakdown of German resistance on VE day,
we were taken from our camp in a British truck convoy
to General Montgomery's headquarters. It was from here,

as space became available, that we were ferried to Brussels, in Dakota aircraft, to be de-loused and sanitized in readiness for going to Britain. British Lancasters flew over the flooded areas of Holland, dropping milk supplies, and then alighted in Brussels for a load of ex-prisoners to transport to Guildford, England. There we were outfitted in khaki by the British to start our homeward journey via London, and Greenoch in Scotland. We arrived back in Canada on May 30th, 1945.

Despite the hardships and the unsanitary conditions, we in Marlag M fared well when compared to other camps elsewhere in Germany housing mostly army types or internees. We had the advantage of being guarded by German navy men whose sense of justice was superior to their SS counterparts. Though my confinement lasted only thirteen months, I can't express in words the elation I felt when it was all over.

17

Escape With A Broken Neck

Jack Leopold

from a taped interview

I was captured at Dieppe in 1942. I had three attempts at escape, the third successful.

In April 1943, about fifty of us got out through a tunnel. Some of us crawled out into a ditch outside the wire and headed into a little town about five or six kilometers away. We managed to get to the railway station, where we thought we would get a train heading east, but it wasn't going east, it was splitting up. We hopped off and headed across a ploughed field. Jimmy Glass and myself, we got pretty far away, but Jimmy Treasdale who had a bum leg got way behind us so we went back; then the Jerries got us; they fired a few shots and we naturally stood still.

They took us into a town about ten kilometers from our camp. They put us into a cell on the railway there and later put us with a bunch of French POWS. They stayed there the rest of the day and the next morning sent guards to pick us up and on the way, well, I guess we may have got a little bit snarly or something like that and they started into us with rifle butts and that is the reason I wear this damn collar now.

My neck was broken, it was what they called ad-jentered — dedenterated discs. They went to powder. The D.V.A. hospital has called me in about three times to operate and fuse them but there is nothing there that would take the fusing. I have to wear this collar. . .

On the second escape we got damned near to Switzerland. We were in a salt car, and anybody in a car full of salt will get a bit thirsty. The train stopped and we hopped down to look for water; the train started to pull away and we just didn't make it. So the Heinies caught us again.

On the third try we were very fortunate: We managed to hit the Yank line. We were marching all over Germany at that time. So we finally said, we are going to get out of here. We were marching at night; in the morning we stop-ped. We saw a big bush. So we snuck out there and duck-ed into the bush and hid overnight waiting for daylight. The next morning there were three other groups plus ourselves who had been hiding from each other all day and night.

This was on Saturday, April 14th, 1945. We holed up in a little barn. The Yanks were too far away to reach; they were shelling and we could see the flash and everything. Then the Jerries came back. They were coming down the little street of this country town, coming down below the front of the barn. We hopped out at the back, about twen-ty feet to the ground, and hid in a big wood pile. The Jer-ries set up a little perimeter outside the town, like on the edges and we decided: "Are we going to stay here in the wood pile, right on the edge of town? We got the perimeter around here, we are going to get whomped anywhere." So we figured we better sneak through — and we did.

We had about five kilometers, I guess, to where the fighting was and we got about half way when it started to get late, so we hid in a ditch, smearing ourselves with mud.

All that was showing were our noses to breathe. The Jerries were coming back and all of a sudden we hear clank, clank, clank. And Keith Waters, he says, "I hear these noises Jack, get up and have a look." So I poked my head up and all I saw was big tanks with white stars on them. And Keith says, "They're my boys." So we got out of the ditch, put our hands up, and everyone on those tanks, they just poured right on us. This is no kidding. And I tell you it was the happiest day in my life.

18

A Wife's Story

Grace Leopold

from a taped interview

Jack and I were married in 1937. Jack joined the forces on September 4th, 1939, and went overseas in June 1940. It was rather a traumatic experience because I was seven months pregnant when he left and I lost the baby nine days later. The doctor imagined it must have been from the worry and the concern. But life had to go on — we already had a two-year old boy — and I went out to work when he was four. I was living with Jack's parents. My mother-in-law was very good and he was well taken care of.

I went to work in a munitions factory, as an inspector of 75 mm shells, which I found very interesting. It made me feel that I was really part of the war effort doing that type of work. I worked there for three years on that project then the government felt that we had enough shells to carry on to the end of the war. So I got other jobs in an office in a big department store and I was again fortunate that people I worked with were very supportive. Even the pharmacist procured all sorts of pamphlets for me to prepare me for the change in my husband when he came home. He said, "You must realize you were very young, twenty, when he left and several years have gone by and people grow up."

I knew Jack's experiences would change him. Of course I had the benefit of Jack's dad's experience — he was also a prisoner in the First World War when Jack was a baby. He knew what it was all about and reassured his mother and me because Jack had a brother who was lost at Dieppe. He had lost one nine months before that in the airforce. So the family realized what war was all about, whereas I didn't.

His dad was a very strong support for both his wife and myself. I don't know what we would have done without him. So I thought that I was very, very fortunate that I had time to prepare myself for the changes. It was hard; you worried, naturally, and especially after the Dieppe raid you'd meet people. There were a few of our boys who got back and I'll never forget one day Jack's mom and I were downtown and this woman said to me: "Now, don't prepare yourself that he is coming home, because my Eugene saw him, he was dead, he was not far from his brother, both the boys are dead." His mother had been notified immediately that Jack's younger brother had been killed at Dieppe, but I was told Jack was missing in action. And I thought well, I don't think I'll need Eugene or anyone else to tell me when Jack's dead, I'll feel it, I'll know it, and the government will inform me. Until then I'm going to believe that he is living. And you just carry on with that. I never, never expected anything to happen to him. I don't know how I would have coped with it if it had, I imagine I would have had to, that's all. But you just had to have faith and hope. And I think that's just how we carried on, most of us. . .

It was very strange how I heard officially that he was a prisoner-of-war. It was through a little postcard that he had somehow smuggled out. It came through Switzerland.

It was December the 8th. All the other people had been notified at the end of October. It was Jack's birthday, in fact. I immediately called the Red Cross, who had been very good, and the gentleman in charge of the Red Cross in Windsor was very, very good to our family. Right away he notified Ottawa. And about three or four days later I got a telegram from Ottawa telling me that they were very happy to inform me that my husband was now a prisoner-of-war. . .

When Jack eventually came back he was very changed. He was very tense, and weighed only one hundred and two pounds. He dropped such a lot of weight, he wasn't the same man. We knew he was going through his experiences and there was the fact that his brothers hadn't come back — they were a very close family. He was the only one who came back, and it must have made a difference, but he didn't express himself much. He seemed to keep everything within him. It's very hard to get him to talk of his experiences. He only really began to talk of his experiences when he got older and mixed with the ex-P.O.W.s, that seemed to draw him out. That's made a great change. The National P.O.W.s' Association has been very beneficial to him.

Our son really didn't know him, other than his picture. He was eight when his dad came back. Of course we had constantly spoken of him, and he had letters and postcards from his father when his dad was able to write. We kept Jack's image in front of him all the time. He was thrilled; he knew his dad the minute he saw him. My dad was down at the station, young Jack on his shoulders, and he jumped right into his own dad's arms. . .

I knew that Jack had tried to escape. When fellows came back, he had warned them not to tell me, but you would talk to them and kind of feel them out and two or three of the boys did tell me. Some of the boys were very upset after that they had told me. They didn't realize it; they'd begin to speak and then they'd start telling you of the experiences and then afterwards we'd feel very down and Jack's father would say, "Well, you know they're upset and they're concerned for him, don't believe it all." He tried to sort of polish it over for us. Having been a prisoner himself he would have had that experience. But that's an extraordinary thing that Jack's father should have been a prisoner, and that he should lose two sons and the third be a prisoner as well.

He knew he could follow Jack on the map. He knew every inch of the step along the way as they started to march, because Mr. Turnbull of the Red Cross would keep us informed and he told us when the camp was liberated. But Jack had escaped four days before, which we didn't know. . .

Jack's done very well since. He's had to give up his usual line of work. He was an iron molder and it was too heavy. He would have probably made more money, but he got into caretaking and education with the Board of Education. Then he got his engineer's certificate. He instructed with the army, stayed with the militia and I think life is pretty much the same as it was then.

He doesn't have good health. We never even had a doctor before he went overseas — he'd never seen a doctor in his life. We don't know how things would have been if he hadn't been there at that age. He's been sick off and on right from the time he came home, periods of hospitalization and so on. But he's been well taken of and he's coped very well with it.

19

A Message From Colonel Noguchi

Alex James

The following notice was circulated through the Chosen Prison Camp in 1942. It is just as it was given in writing to prisoners coming into camp complete with all the mistakes in spelling.

"Instruction given by Colonel Y. Noguchi, Superintendent of The Chosen War Prisoners' Camp.

September 26th 1942

(It is requested that you should preserve these papers after having read through.)

I am Colonel Y. Noguchi, Superintendent of the Chosen War Prisoners' Camp. Receiving you here, I should like to give necessary instruction to you all.

I hope you will consider how this Greater East Asia War happened. Nippons desired for peaceful settlement arising from the conciliatory spirit, rejected by America and Britain in order to attain their ambitious demand to East Asia. Finally they overwhelmed Nippon, the important defenser of Asia, to the extent that they dared to resort to violence of economic disruption.

Promoting Chinese internal confusion and increasing military preparation on all sides of Nippon Empire to challenge us, thus the very existence of our nation being in danger, we stood up resolutely with unity of will, strong as iron, under the name of Tenno (Emperor) for the emancipation of the nations and elimination of evil sources in East Asia.

The rise or fall of our Empire that has the glorious history and the progress or decline depend upon the present war. Firm and unshakable is our national resolve, that we should crush our enemy the U.S.A. and the Britain.

Heaven is always on the side of Justice. Within ten days after the War Declaration, our Navy and Naval Air Forces annihilated both the American Pacific fleet and British long established Army, Navy, and Air Bases were crushed by our Army and Army Air Forces; and now, tide turning in our favour, all parts of regions linked with Burma, Java, and Wake Island have already been occupied by us, and the inhabitants there are rejoicing in cooperation with us for the construction of New Asia. And now these above facts have induced the Indian rebellion and Australia come to a cricis of capture. Afterward our belligerants sent their air crafts and fleets for the rescue, but every time they were sunk to the bottom or destroyed and repulsed, thus the total damages come up to 2801 vessels and 4500 Air crafts.

I think these war results do not signify the inferior power of our enemy, but rather owe to our absolute indomitable power — that is to say the power, protected by Kami (Heaven). Wherever Nippon Army and Navy advance, Tenyu Shinjo (Special Providencial Help) always follows; you should recognize the fact and consider the reasons.

Nippon Army and Navy are under the Imperial Command of Tenno (Emperor) who is the personification of Kami (God), so that the Imperial troops are to be called the troops of God. Now you have become war prisoners because of struggling against Kami-no-Gun (God's Army) and now you are convinced of fearfulness to the marrow and became aware of unsavourly results. What do you think of this?

However you have lost fighting strength now, you once fought fiercely against us. Judging from this fact some of you will hold hostile feeling against us in your hearts that can never be permission. Accordingly, we will punish you if you act against our regulations, for instance the non-fulfilment of regulations, disobedience, resistance and escape (even an attempt to do so) are understood as manifestation of hostility.

I kindly requested you that you must be cautious not spoiling yourselves by punishment.

But on the other hand, with Nippon warrior's forgiveness I express respect to your faithfulness to your country and fulfilment of your duty, and feel pitiful for your capitulation after exhaustion.

You should reflect on yourselves. According to the extend of your malice feeling we also put certain limit to your freedom you enjoy or severity and lenity on your treatment.

Parols is of use as a proof of wiping away your hostility. I am regretful to say those refused to swear will be treated as persons of enemy character, will be placed under restraint regarding maintenance of honour, protection of your persons and must endure pain in compensation of hostility.

The details of conctrete outline of style of daily life are defined in "The regulation regarding to daily life"; you should put them into practice strictly after reading them over.

Prejudice against labour and grumbling over food, clothing and housing are strictly prohibited, because the change in your daily life and custom are inevitable under present war situation.

Closing my instruction, I advise you all to find interest

and anxiety in your forthcoming daily life by acting according the Imperial military discipline.

20

Rome Organization

H.J. (Barney) Byrnes

Italy surrendered to the Allies September 8th, 1945. On that date some seven thousand Allied prisoners-of-war were confined in Italian camps under Italian guards. For the most part the guards downed tools and went home, leaving the inmates to saunter out into the surrounding country. A few camps were taken over immediately by German troops and prisoners loaded on trains for Germany but, avoiding recapture, over three-quarters spread out over the countryside. For many, Rome, with the apparent sanctuary of the Vatican, became the target city.

During their slow and clandestine approach to the city, they were sheltered and fed by country and village folk, parish priests, and tradesmen, partisans, hookers, and blackmarketeers. As this tide of evaders converged on the city, messages began to arrive at the British Legation to the Holy See, by this time interned within the Vatican, giving names and locations together with requests for maintenance or sanctuary in the Vatican.

The Vatican would not nor could not take in this ragged and destitute flood. Extra guards were mounted and stringent admittance rules adopted. Of the hundreds who tried to enter, only thirteen were able to sneak in and gain internment status. The rest could not be abandoned, nor were they, as a zany, haphazard aggregation of priests and laity rushed to provide hidden shelter and maintenance.

Known simply as the Rome Organization, it was born of a meeting of three concerned men, an Irish Monsignor, Hugh O'Flaherty, the British Minister to the Holy See, Sir D'Arcy Osborne and the Legation butler, John May. It had no table of organization, no definite rank structure nor, at first, a sure source of funds, but it did have dedication, enthusiasm and the unwavering support of Italians in all walks of life.

During the period September 1943 to early June 1944 the Rome Organization sheltered and maintained three hundred escapees in the City of Rome and roughly three thousand within a fifty-mile radius of the city.

The bulk of the infiltrators into Rome were quartered in some of the extra-territorial buildings belonging to the Vatican and scattered throughout the city. A few apartments were rented as temporary clearing houses until other accommodation could be found. The latter were private households ranging from the very poor to the very wealthy. In fact, you were not considered to be anyone socially if your circle wasn't aware that you had one or more escapees hidden in the house.

At first, funds were obtained by loans or as outright gifts from wealthy Romans, but once the operation got under way, British Foreign Office funds materialized.

Of the three Founding Fathers, O'Flaherty, Osborne and May, O'Flaherty with his wide circle of acquaintances raised funds, organized a priestly web of communications, located billets, and supplied much of the drive and enthusiasm of the project. Sir D'Arcy Osborne, nominal head of Rome Organization, was the vital link with the UK source of funds. John May, butler and scrounger extraordinary, knew the principal black marketeers and could supply almost anything required.

Food was rationed and scarce. The Swiss, in control of the Red Cross parcel warehouse, could and did make these stores available. Worn-out footwear was a problem until a contract shoe repairer working for the German Army was discovered next door to a sympathetic neutral embassy. It then became routine for battered boots to be exchanged by midnight requisition.

The Organization had one British Medical Officer excapee and a young civilian medical student. A dental officer escapee turned up and was equipped with an emergency kit.

A burst-appendix operation was performed in a German-controlled hospital without detection, the naked, anaesthetized and blanketed patient delivered, operated on and spirited away to a safe house — simple, how could anyone tell the nationality of a naked unconscious patient?

During the first few months the enemy made but few attempts to round up escapees and as long as a low profile was maintained, it was possible to move about the city undetected. This situation changed early in 1944 when raids cost the Organization both helpers and evaders. A counter tactic was the discovery of a sympathizer in the Questura. Here raids were planned and committed to paper one day ahead. The Questura friend obligingly put an extra carbon in his typewriter, which carbon found its way to the Organization in time to move those threatened.

In the Fall of 1943, Sir D'Arcy, deciding that the scope of the operation and the numbers involved demanded a more military structure, arranged for Major Sam Derry to be brought to Rome. Sam at that time was in charge of a large group of evaders in a village a few miles outside the city. Sam was to organize and administer a situation becoming daily more difficult to manage by civilians. He was accordingly smuggled into the Vatican and with the assistance of two Italian-speaking British subalterns, Bill Simpson and

John Furman, was able to bring order and some discipline to young men beginning to chafe at their hidden and restricted lives.

By late Spring, 1944, with food becoming scarcer and safe billets harder to find, every effort was made to keep evaders from drifting to Rome. In the country, living was safer and country people always had some food they were prepared to share with their uninvited but welcome guests.

In early June, the end of Rome's travail was plain to see. German troops began to leave the city and the people to ignore the seven o'clock curfew. On June 4th, the clangour of church bells pulled a frantically happy population into the streets as the first Allied troops entered the city.

The Rome Organization dissolved itself and the principals were faced with the question, "How can the efforts and the sacrifices of Italian helpers be recognized."

Penalties for helping escaped prisoners had been severe. Heads of families had been shot. Others had been imprisoned or sent to labour camps in Germany. Houses had been burned and livestock run off. Despite German and Fascist round-ups, Italian helpers sheltered our escapees when the penalties for detection were horrendous, fed them when food was scarce, clothed them when clothing was irreplaceable, provided bicycles and boats, guided and assisted them in every way to move on toward Switzerland or the seacoast, or simply to lie low and await our advancing forces. There was no way in which the Rome Organization founders could walk away and leave these people without so much as a thank you.

This view was shared by the Allied Powers. The Allied Screening Commission was established with a mandate to award due recognition for assistance rendered, wherever possible to repay debts incurred and again where possible, to pay compensation for damages, loss and injury resulting from activities in assistance to evaders.

The work of the Allied Screening Commission commenced on June 5th, 1944, the first official day of the liberation of Rome. Strength consisted of the four officers of Rome Organization and a volunteer typist. During the months that followed and with the assistance given by the UK, the Commonwealth and the USA, numbers grew to over two hundred including civilian help. With detachments in principal cities, the task of the Allied Screening Commission was completed by the end of September, 1947. By that time, ninety thousand cases of help rendered were investigated and one million pounds sterling expended in compensation. Seventy-five thousand official Certificates of Thanks were issued and a variety of services provided for helpers. These services were varied in character including the finding of jobs, early repatriation of sons and husbands held in Allied POW camps, treatment of sick and injured in Allied hospitals, transport of helpers' families when no transport was available to civilians, even to the provision of soccer uniforms and equipment to a boys' school which had sheltered Allied evaders throughout the German occupation and which would accept no other compensation.

The Allied Powers owed a debt to the citizen helpers of Rome and of all of Italy. The Allied Screening Commission did its best to see that the debt was acknowledged.

*   *   *   *

Editor's note: Barney Byrnes, the only Canadian member of the Rome Organization, was captured in Sicily July 24th, 1943 He was held in Campo Concentramento PG 66 near Capua, escaped and by means of an inattentive guard and a temporarily open gate, slipped into the Vatican. There he was officially interned until the fall of Rome, in June 1944. During his internment he was engaged in the paper work and general administration of the Rome Organization. He also served as C.O. Allied Screening Commission, from the fall of 1944 until repatriated to Canada in early summer, 1945.

The story of the Rome Organization has been told in these books:

Be Not Fearful, John Furman
Rome Escape Line, S. I. Derry
Scarlet Pimpernel of the Vatican, J. P. Gallagher

It was also televised in part in the mini-series *The Scarlet and the Black* during the fall of 1983.

Left to right: John Furman, Sam Derry, Barney Byrnes, Bill Simpson.

21

Red Cross To The Rescue

Harry Smith
from a taped interview

The end of the war in Europe was approaching when a dozen of us left Stalag-VII A under escort for the Swiss border. We went to Lake Constance where our group was divided into two separate parties under two German officers. Apart from the Canadians, we included a New Zealander and an Australian Regimental Sergeant Major. He was, in fact, English but had emigrated to Australia and had joined the Australian army and acquired his rank there. There were also a German officer, a sergeant, a corporal, and two private soldiers, acting as protectors in the event that we had differences with more militant Germans or, particularly, the SS. The whole convoy was under the charge of the Swiss delegate.

We also had with us three Swiss nurses; one of them, Sister Agnes, was a very intelligent woman who had been engaged in social work and working with refugees for a number of years. She spoke excellent English and it was my privilege to have her riding with me at times. She was a help to me, since my knowledge of German was rather limited although I could get by.

We left Constance sometime after dark, travelled for a few miles and then stopped in a little village where we slept the best way we could in our trucks.

We had four or five Swiss drivers with us, civilians, who took turns driving. We carried on that day, travelled down through southern Bavaria and eventually hit the main highway, Munich to Vienna. We went through Salzburg, going south to Stalag XVIII-C. We had a big load of Red Cross parcels. While we were going past a railway marshalling yard, we were caught in an air-raid. A number of bombs dropped on the railway. The first thing I heard were loud explosions and, looking back, saw rails and box-cars going up in the air. The chap ahead of me, a Swiss driver, lost his cool, stopped his truck and jumped out. The other driver jumped with him and they headed for bush and open ground away from the highway. The planes made a circle and dumped some more bombs. They were short of their target and just missed us. Even so, we holed up for two or three hours.

Eventually, we carried on and reached a prison camp, where there were quite a number of Americans and a large number of Russian prisoners. They were all in desperate straits for food, the Russians particularly. They weren't members of the Geneva Convention so they received no parcels whatever. The Americans and the other Allied prisoners who were there held a meeting and decided that since the Russians were in such a sorry plight, they would pool whatever resources and food they had and help them. It was a noble gesture on their part because they weren't on full rations by a long shot. Many of the Russians weren't accustomed to our way of living and to things like canned foods, and some of them didn't know how to open the cans. I saw one Russian carrying a quarter-pound tin of tea which he'd had for several days and hadn't opened. Probably didn't know what it was.

After the convoy was unloaded, we went via Linz to an infamous concentration camp, Mauthausen.

Even though many of us had been in prison for from one year to four, none of us knew very much about these camps. It seemed to be a well-guarded secret. Even talking to men who had been working on what we called "Kommandos", moving from place to place during that portion of the war — they didn't know much about them. We did know that certain prisoners, particularly political offenders, were consigned to these places and were put out on working parties, because we used to see them in Munich. But we didn't know about the atrocities until we arrived at Mauthausen.

The first thing we saw was a group of Russian women. They were working on a gravel pit and were loading gravel with shovels out of the railway cars. Most of us, being Canadians, were quite incensed, because we didn't treat *our* women in that manner.

There were two German women hanging from a tree near the entrance to the camp. They had been hanged by the SS for stealing bread rations. And then we began to hear things whispered about when we got to the main camp. When we brought out one hundred and fifteen French women and about ten or twelve French men, one or two who spoke English said, "We won't tell you what's been happening in there because you wouldn't believe us."

Incidentally, the Germans wouldn't allow any of us into the camp itself. Myself and another chap had to go up to the main prison gate with our trucks to bring out some stretcher cases — women who had been hurt in an air-raid and others who had more or less lost their minds. There we turned the trucks over to two Russian prisoners who drove them into the prison. We had to sit and wait in the guardroom.

We heard the story of a British paratrooper who had been dragged in there behind a car. His wrists were tied together. When they arrived at the camp, he got to his feet and they untied him and he just laughed in their faces. It was generally believed that he was taken out and shot because no one ever heard of him after that.

One of the Swiss nurses was with me; she sat beside me in the guardroom and was frightened — the SS were tough-looking characters. We got away during that afternoon and were two days getting back to the Swiss border. At night, when we stopped, the refugees bedded down and slept wherever they could. There were two trucks loaded with stretcher cases — women's stretcher cases. Two of them were English, well-to-do women who had been spending their holidays in Germany at the outbreak of war. They were women who had led a life of, maybe not luxury, but ease at any rate. One was the wife of a moving-picture producer. They had been interned and eventually put into this concentration camp. One of them was completely bedridden and the other bedridden up to a certain point, but they were sane enough and they took things just like most of the British did. They didn't worry too much.

Eventually we arrived back at the Swiss border. The French women with us had been rounded up indiscriminately by the Germans, who had wanted people to go to work and just rounded up anybody. Some were from good families accustomed to a good life; others were more or less streetwalkers, but they were all women and they were all grateful that we were able to get them out because they had been ultimately headed for the gas chambers. They didn't have anything to eat, and we had to show discretion in our own eating and snacking. We didn't have too many stops where we could make up a good meal but we had rations with us. When we made coffee, at infrequent opportunities, I used to take a cup around to the French nurse who was looking after the women in my truck.

When we arrived at the Swiss border we had the usual hassle with the SS. They didn't want us to deliver the people into Switzerland. There was a German guard, Austrian actually, and when he heard there were some Canadians in the convoy he dropped everything and ran over to visit us. He had lived in Nova Scotia for a number of years.

Finally, everything worked out all right. We said good-bye to our French prisoners and then waited for several days until another convoy showed up. There were ten trucks, French-built Renaults, weighing about a ton and a half. The front wheels were built out flush with the outside duals.

Again we set out with a load of invalid parcels, headed for Dachau. These parcels were intended for people who were on the verge of starvation. When we reached our destination, there was a hassle again with the SS. They didn't want to accept the parcels and there were some SS out on the parade square, more or less drunk, and shipping everybody they could up to the front line. While we were there a group of Polish Jews was brought in. I don't know how long they had marched. There were twenty women with them, some carrying babes in their arms. Most were in a sorry state, starved, ragged, tired, some so badly gone they were being dragged along in blankets. If they dropped out, the guards would shoot them, and that was the end of them. I recall a German soldier throwing a bit of meat and bread in among the group. I don't know whether he did it for sport or not, but they were fighting over it, and they were so weak that when they struck one another I'm quite sure they didn't feel it. They'd strike a man so hard and yet there was no force in the blow.

Eventually the Swiss drivers were allowed to take the trucks in and when they came out they were still shaking. They said, "We're not going to tell you what we saw in there."

That was the day before the Americans went through. After that the full story hit the front pages.

22

View From A Younger Generation

Jonathan Vance

When first approached to make a contribution to this book, I must admit I was rather surprised. It seemed rather ironic for me in my late teens, to be writing for ex-prisoners, some of whom were old enough to be my grandfather, after I had been badgering them to write for me for so many years. However, it is only fair that I should reciprocate, and perhaps explain why I had been doing this since about 1975.

It remains a mystery to me why I became interested in the subject of prisoners-of-war in the first place. My mother, who had an interest in POWs before I was born, maintains that it is genetic. I began my study in earnest after seeing the movie *The Great Escape* for the first time; I was greatly impressed by the ingenuity, cleverness and courage of the men involved. For the first while, my study centred on a small group of escapees and their exploits. It was a constant source of amazement to me that they managed to concoct so many varied and unlikely escape schemes. At times, I was shocked by their audacity.

Gradually, though, I became more and more aware of

the average prisoner, the one who didn't achieve notorie-
ty with numerous daring escape attempts. I became deeply impressed by the courage of these men, courage of a
different kind. Courage to exist through interminable hours
of boredom and seemingly endless repetition. Courage to
maintain their personal views, and to help others maintain
their own, under tremendous pressure. Courage to attack
the enemy whenever the opportunity presented itself, and
in any way to keep them off balance. Though less spec-
tacular than the courage of the great escaper, it is certainly
no less easy to maintain.

It is with this average prisoner that I have had the most
contact in my study. An ex-rifleman in New Zealand, a
financial magnate in Toronto and a peer of the realm in
Scotland have all responded to my requests. In these and
many other responses, I have come across many varied at-
titudes to my study. Some are quite astonished to hear that
someone still cares after so many years; others are delighted
that someone is taking it upon himself to preserve their
stories; some are genuinely tired of people trying to pry
into their past; others believe that there could be nothing
in anyone's captivity that deserves remembering.

However, there is one belief that is common to most
men I have contacted, the belief that their own conduct
in prison was nothing special, and deserves no special place
in history. This is where I disagree; in the over seven years
that I have been studying the subject, I have not come across
a single story that did not deserve to be preserved. They
all contain some special details, details which underline
the true courage of the men involved. Of course, those men
see nothing particularly heroic in their actions, but a kind
of heroism is apparent to the impartial observer like myself.

Studying prisoners-of-war has been an immensely
valuable and broadening experience for me. It is a wonderful feeling to put down on paper a story that might otherwise have been lost. Not only have I come across many
valuable stories, but I've also met many fascinating peo-

ple. The multiple escapee who became a professor of veterinary surgery and the commando who became a major international law enforcement officer both gave their assistance freely and fully. As long as there are men willing to tell their stories, I will be more than willing to listen to them and preserve them.

23

The Kaiser's War

Alfred Cleeton

from a taped interview

I was born on August 17th, 1892 in a small town called Hednesford about fifteen miles outside of Birmingham. I went to public school and when I was fourteen I felt the same as other boys do at fourteen, I wanted a job to have some money of my own. The first job was working in a men's ready-to-wear store, next in the pay office of a mining company.

I was there for about two years and wrote my Oxford Junior at the Midland Institute in Birmingham when I was sixteen. By the time I was seventeen I was back at school as a pupil-teacher. That didn't satisfy me, so I next found employment in an office in Birmingham with the now defunct London and North Western Railway.

In June 1913 I went to Liverpool, boarded a vessel for Montreal and travelled by train, the old fashioned CPR train, no upholstery on the seats, just plain boards and a blanket. I went straight through to Rossland in British Columbia where my father had been for some years. On July 9th that same year I was on the payroll with the Canadian Pacific Railway Company. Everything worked well, I liked the work, I enjoyed myself. Started out at sixty dollars a month, twelve hours a day from 6 a.m. to 6 p.m., three hundred and sixty-five days a year. No time off for Sundays. You never heard of Labour Day or Christmas Day or any other day. Every day was the same to the CPR.

The war broke out in August 1914. By this time I was approaching my twenty-second birthday and I joined up early in August and left Rossland with a unit set up by two retired English soldiers who between them gathered together one hundred and sixty men from the West Kootenay area: Nelson, Trail, Grand Forks and Rossland. Major Rigby and his unit left Rossland on August 28th, bound for Quebec where we became attached to the 12th Quebec Rosslands. We went overseas as the first Canadian division. Thirty-six sailing ships loaded from stem to stern with civilians in civilian dress headed for a war. We trained for a short time with the Quebec Rifles, which at that time were unitized as the 12th Canadian Infantry Battalion. When we reached England we made for Salisbury Plain, that small part of the world known for its sticky mud.

We had travelled over on the *Scotian*. We eventually reached Salisbury Plain and were billeted at a place known as Pond Farm; it was well named. While we were at Pond Farm Major Rigby had made enquiries about trying to become a part of a regiment from British Columbia known as the First British Columbia Regiment. He succeeded in getting us attached to this unit and we trained then with the First B.C. Regiment, later to become the Seventh Canadian Infantry Battalion.

When we trained thirty miles a day was considered a normal hike. But there were days when it was impossible to be out because of the weather. On those occasions we had to take to the theory of war and the theory of learning how to get the other fellow before he got you, so that our days and nights were completely occupied with training of one sort or another pertaining to the military.

After leaving the French coast we marched to a place in Belgium called Ploegsteert. We were billeted in a shelled-out brewery in a vat which held fifty-six men. We were so tired by the time we got there we didn't know where to make beds so we just fell over the top of the vat down into bales of hay and straw, kit bag for a pillow and over-coat for a blanket. And we slept till the following morning.

Our kit at that time consisted of a rolled-up piece of material which held your razor, your comb and brush, your toothbrush, your toothpaste and all the necessary things such as needles and cotton and a few pins and so on. Then of course you had in addition to your wearing apparel a suit of underwear, and an extra pair of socks and an extra shirt. You had your rifle, bayonet, and one hundred and fifty rounds of ammunition. The rifle we used up to my time of capture was the Ross rifle, which was the most useless tool that was ever handed to a man under war conditions. It was a fine gun for target work, but for trench warfare it was a complete washout. You never knew when it was go-ing to kick back at you and you never knew when it was going to give in and work with you.

They moved us from Ploegsteert, which we called Plug Street, to Fleur Bais and from Fleur Bais we moved onto the Ypres front.

Now the Ypres front could best be described as a quart bottle with a long neck. This part of the line had been held by French Senegalese troops, the boys with the red pants and the long wide-flowing overcoats. Incidentally, we lost our Major Rigby at Fleur Bais when, probably in a loose moment of inner tension, he stuck his head a few inches above the parapet instead of using the periscope to see what was happening along the German front. At the time they were only one hundred and fifty to two hundred yards from our line. So it was a matter of rifle shooting and machine gun work. He no sooner popped his head above the top of the parapet when he got a bullet from a German rifle right smack between the eyes. Just removed his foot from me. A little place he dug in the bottom of the sand bag, just laid down and he was gone. Major Rigby was a model soldier, wonderful man.

We were moved over to Ypres quite early in April. Our billets there, where we slept, were just a farm house with the outer building and not two bricks standing on each other anywhere. The wooden building had been completely demolished by shell fire and the brick buildings were so badly knocked about that you could see horses' hooves and horses' tails and parts of their heads sticking out through the razed buildings.

On the afternoon of April 22nd I was sitting outside on a heap of rubble, buildings that had been knocked over. I had just finished writing a letter to my mother and one to my girl-friend who I later married. By five o'clock I was ready to get over to the company mailbox when I perceived the sky filling rapidly with a greenish-yellow substance. This could be no other than chlorine gas which had been so minutely described to us in lectures on Salisbury Plain and at billets in France. I screamed my head off as did many others, giving the alarm. Our platoon managed to herd into an underground cellar which held fifty-six men. We were already in light marching order. At nine that night Captain Lott, second-in-command of Number Two Company, came along and kicked in a very small pane of glass and snorted out the order. "Number Eight Platoon, Lieutenant Steves, fall in in single file outside at 2100". That was now.

They started us off on a march, single file, three paces apart, until somewhere around three in the morning the command was passed along to halt, right turn, dig in, take advantage of all cover. So with those little shovels that we had we really had a day's work to do in two hours.

By the time daylight broke most of the fellows had just enough cover to put their head in. From there on they had to work with hands and feet and that little shovel, until by mid-day they were getting their shoulder covered, the upper part of the body; the idea being that you had to avoid breathing chlorine gas if possible, because on our way up to the lines we had walked over hundreds of dead bodies where they had been caught with the full force of the gas.

We were up there until the following morning when platoon commanders sent out scouts to find out why our artillery was dropping the shells short.

By noon on the 23rd we began to realize, and so did everyone who happened to be capable of thinking and putting two and two together and determining from the direction the shells were coming from, that we were pretty well covered on four sides. The Germans were using our own artillery to drop into our pocket. We put up with this until Saturday morning under the command that this position had to be held at all costs.

The German trick was to follow the gas as closely as conditions permitted. By Saturday morning we could hear their bands playing. We had nothing except a few cans of hard-tack to eat and a small amount of water. Every platoon in the 7th Battalion made a detail of whatever men were available to bring in water from one pump that hadn't been shelled; but it was two miles away and we had a rough time to crawl through the brush and mud as well as the remains of the gas. Nobody was volunteering from our platoon so our platoon sergeant decided he would ask us to come up in alphabetical order. A friend of mine was a chap named Bailey, who spoke French fluently. Bailey and Cleeton were the first two to go up. It was a case of crawling on your belly for two miles with empty bottles, fourteen bottles each, slung over our two shoulders. We got back without any problems. But the shelling continued and it was taking its toll in our own line. We also had to contend with the gas that was slowly clearing.

We'd lost our colonel on the night of the 22nd, also our company commander, and of course we had lost our Major Rigby in Fleur Bais, so we were in more or less a state of flux. Nobody quite knew who was who under those conditions.

The word was passed along that we would have to retire two hundred yards to a support-trench behind us, which other troops had prepared while we were up in the head end. In the early afternoon the Germans came in in full force: cavalry, infantry, and you could hear the bands playing.

I don't quite know where or how I got mine, but it was probably that sprint out in the front line into the support trench. It took a piece of my leg from just below the left knee, which made it almost impossible to attempt to crawl away, never mind anything else. I had used my own emergency bandage and there was so much disorder it was completely out of the question to try to arrange anything normal in your own mind under those conditions.

The next thing I knew I woke up with my overcoat over my face and somebody had cut the leg out of my underwear and out of my pants on my left leg and cut my shoe off. I was surrounded by numerous German troops. They wheeled me into a field dressing-station behind their own lines and then into a large building. There I lay for two or three days. On my right was a chap named Edward Gyde, who belonged to the 7th Battalion and on my left, lying on the floor, was an older man, must have been in his late thirties or forties, named Richards, who belonged to the Rifle Brigade from London. So you can tell what a mixed up kettle of fish it was. This chap Richards died during that first night. Gyde had been hit in the back and out the front with a piece of shrapnel. He was in poor shape.

We had no treatment at all. They just took the bandage off and put another on and tied it up and away you went.

They put us on the train and we landed at a place called Paderborn, where we went into a priest's seminary for medical treatment. Inside the main entrance they had a large number of empty wooden tubs. Every man was wounded, of course; they didn't have an able-bodied man in the bunch with two legs, two arms and two eyes. Nevertheless, a couple of big Germans picked me up and dropped me into one of the tubs which was full of boiling hot water. You could smell the salt. Of course all the bandage came off. They took our uniforms away and we never saw them again. I remember my cap had been riddled with bullet holes. Just the ordinary cap; we didn't have the service cap those days.

From Paderborn they took us to a camp in Westphalia named Sennelager, near Munster. At Sennelager there were four camps in one; it was a huge area divided into four. When we left the hospital it was in wagons drawn by prisoners-of-war. Depending on the size of the wagon there would be anything from twelve to sixteen men with a rope around their shoulders slipped onto a hook on the side of the wagon. The German cavalry was all in use at the front.

I was the only Canadian in that particular wagon. As soon as we reached the camp they dropped us off at the gates. There were hundreds of German sentries on duty at the entrances to the four different camps. Three men approached me and wanted to know my name, where I was from and all about it. They took me into their group, men joined together to make sure that everybody had a bite to eat. Every parcel that came into that group was put on the floor and each one had his share at each meal.

But of course it took months before your own Red Cross parcels arrived. Meanwhile you had only the German rations, which consisted of a small piece of black bread in the morning and a bowl of something that was wet and hot at noon and then a piece of sausage and another piece of bread about as big as the palm of your hand at night. There was all the water you could drink, of course, but there was very little hot water to be had anytime. If you wanted to take a bath, it was in cold water.

The camps included all nationalities: Chinese, Japanese, Russians, French, Hungarian, Montenegrins and

Servians. Among our few fellows who had left Rossland there were three Montenegrins, the finest fellows you'd ever wish to meet, big, strong, muscular men. They'd worked in the mines. These three boys took me in. By this time I'd had my twenty-second birthday, in August 1915, and they looked after me well and truly. The first thing they said was "Do you smoke?", and I said, "Oh, anything I can get under these conditions." And they said, "Can you use a pipe?" and I said I'd used a pipe for years. I had of course, as a kid learned to smoke at fifteen. So they dug out an old pipe and filled it with some Bruno flake and handed it to me. Then they gave me a bite to eat; they had some biscuits and a little bit of French bread. They got one loaf every two weeks, and it used to take three weeks to get it from Switzerland up into Westphalia.

The life at Sennelager was an extremely unhappy one for all concerned. It was a situation whereby a man had to have a very strong mind and he had to have a determination built in that he was only there for a short time, that it couldn't last. So it was a matter of not only from day to day but from hour to hour. There were lists posted daily on men who were being sent out all over Germany, Austria and Hungary, out to different camps and working parties, farm parties. Everybody wanted to get on a farm.

There were working parties every day. Nobody was left in camp, only those who reported for the sick parade, and if you reported for the sick parade and you weren't sick you'd better watch out because you were going to get your backside kicked from one side of the block to the other. Those who were really sick invariably got a "number nine." That was the only medical inspection we got. I never saw a doctor in that camp from the time I went in until the time I came out.

Late in 1915 there was a man in Number Two block at Sennelager, a chap named Victor Champion who belonged to the First Lancashire Regiment. He'd been a drummer in the armoury, an intelligent sort of chap, well built. You could tell he had lived an extremely clean life; it showed on the outside, and under conditions like I lived for forty months you didn't have to go to an elementary school nor a secondary school nor a university to be able to measure a man when you met him. You had something, you developed something under those conditions, both a mental and a physical condition that spelled either success or ruin. It had to be one or the other, there was no mid way between the two.

This chap, Champion, was one of the finest men I ever met in my life. I hadn't been in camp very long before I heard rumours going around that they were going to start a sing-song on a Sunday afternoon if it could be arranged through the Kommandant, even if it was outside in the summer or in one of the rooms in the wintertime and bad weather, but they had to have permission anyway. And so Champion begged permission through the Senior Non-commissioned Officer, a Company Sergeant-Major Bentley. There had to be a Senior N.C.O. in every camp who was responsible for the proper conduct of the men under his charge. Champion made contact with a messenger who came from the General's office, General Ian Steinecker. This chap whom General Steinecker sent to interview Victor Champion and Sergeant-Major Bentley had been a practising lawyer in London, England, before the war broke out. He had just got out in time; he knew what was coming, he was a well-educated man, highly intelligent, one of the few Germans I saw who was not savage. He was a small man who spoke perfect English and French. He wasn't fat or big like a pot-bellied German. So Champion saw the picture right away, and he worked on this chap and got all kinds of favours.

Now first of all we had to have money to buy lumber.

We all chipped in, probably eight thousand of us. Some were getting their money from England, you see. We were getting a dollar a day from the Germans; wooden money expendable only in the camp. It was absolutely useless outside the camp. Anyway, Champion worked on this man, to the extent that ostensibly they became firm friends. Champion got lumber and nails and permission to run this hymn sing on a Sunday afternoon. He had another man named Walter Reed who played a little organ that we bought. Walter Reed played the organ and Victor Champion led the singing. In my earlier days I had done some vocal work too. I was one of Champion's first helpers. We got seats made out of two by sixes and one by eights and we used to have a real time there for a couple of hours on a Sunday.

On Sunday too they used to allow boxing, but no gloves. You weren't allowed to strip, only to your underwear.

In the fall of 1915 this group of mine was included in a number of men who were being sent out to various farms. Now it never occurred to us to ask the question "Why a farm in December?" If we could just get away from Sennelager it meant a possibility of a chance to get on the move. Escape, no compass or anything; you made your own way the best way you could. You walked at night and lay up in the daytime. This was the generally established rule for those who could make it.

In our group, there were four of us listed with a number of other men who were being sent on. A man named Snowden defaulted, saying he was going to book sick, they could kick hell out of him from A to Z if they wished, but he said, "I'm not leaving this camp as long as I can stay in it. Especially in the wintertime."

So he stayed, but the other two and I went along. I

couldn't tell you how many people there were at work on this place where we stopped. We had left the camp on the 21st of December and we disembarked from the train on the morning of the 23rd and had been travelling all the way. Just one crust of bread and a bucket of water put in a car with forty men. We got off the train, disembarking at a place called Horde. Horde was in the Dortmund area, the largest munitions area next to Essen. When we disembarked and got our feet on the ground all we could see was chimney stacks, huge affairs belching black smut into the sky.

The men were divided up; fifteen of us managed to have a quick consultation, only for a matter of a minute or so, and the key word was "no work here." We decided there and then. We had learned a few wrinkles during some of the wettest and rainiest days on Salisbury Plain about the conditions meted out to prisoners-of-war, that under war conditions prisoners could not be forced to work in German factories that were supplying munitions to the enemy. So of course we adopted the German words, "nix arbeit," no work, and it didn't take long before we found out that we had made a mistake as far as everything except principle was concerned. But we stuck by the principle; we didn't intend to work. A great big German gave me a boot in the backside and almost threw me onto one of the cars that I had to push that was loaded with empty shells that were being moved to where they were being loaded. We stuck together as we could; all fifteen of us refused to work. For two days the Germans did nothing but use the bayonet on us, or the butt end of a rifle. You got up and they'd strike you across the back of the neck or across the shoulders with the butt end. They had the bayonet to play with at the other end, and if you didn't get up when they began to kick you they began to stick you with the bayonet.

They kept the fifteen of us together because we couldn't speak French, we couldn't speak German, we couldn't speak anything but English. We had no intention of learning, either. Most of us had picked up a little here and there and I know I had my share and simply because I had a little better education than some of the boys I could determine the difference between right and wrong. I could smell a rat. But we took a very severe beating. They used every form of punishment they could devise. The last chance of getting us to work was to stand us up in one corner of the plant away from everywhere else, as far away as they could get us. There were thousands of Russians in the plant at Horde; there were tens of thousands of Russians and Frenchmen, to say nothing of the Japanese and the Italians.

There was a board fence eight feet high and you were lined up three paces part and you were stood there and they told you in German to stand erect, toes at an angle of forty-five degrees, thumbs in line with the seams on your pants. The pants were prison garb, a black material with a big three-inch stripe all down the pants and the sleeves of the coat and down the back of the jacket. They stood us up there from five o'clock in the morning until ten o'clock at night, fifteen of us.

On one occasion one of our number, MacArthur, who was wearing a British Warm, felt his nose running. Of course he couldn't do anything about it. Even if you wanted to go to the bathroom there was no moving, you performed your business right there and that was that. So he hinted; he just turned his head, that was all. A German struck him across the back of the neck. MacArthur jumped, and of course there were a dozen there, but he did have time to open his British Warm and say, "Here, you bastard, put it here, stick it here." That was the last I heard of Jack MacArthur, the last I saw. We all went down eventually. Finally I collapsed too. I don't how many were left, I think there were two or three when they carried me out. They couldn't do a thing at all for me. They put me on a train and sent me back to Sennelager. Where the others went or whether they died, I don't know, I never saw a one after that day. They sent me back to Sennelager and they put me into the hospital, a barn with a concrete floor and a bale of hay and one blanket. I was there from the 24th of December until the 6th of February.

From the 7th of February until the end of July I was sick with double pneumonia. I never saw a doctor, I never saw a nurse, I never had a pill. The only individual I saw was Vic Champion. The German interpreter had issued an order that Champion was allowed to go to the hospital to visit me. Champion came over several times while I was in there. The last time I saw him he knelt by that bale of hay by my side, and he says "Fred, can you hear me?", and I nodded, and he said "How are they treating you?" and I just nodded. I couldn't tell him that the only medical attention I had was a Frenchman with three stripes up who came in one morning and plunged a syringe first in the one side and then in the other. Champion came in one day and a German told him that the Frenchman had said, "This boy is not for long." So Vic took my dogtag and sent it to my mother. Finally at the end of July, they sent me back to Sennelager. I went in a wagon, drawn by our fellows. They used these wagons normally for hauling the mail into the camp from the post office two miles away. There were sixteen men to a wagon. They got sores all over their shoulders from the harness. Anyway, I went back into the camp in July and by this time Vic Champion had talked the Germans into all kinds of concessions. They'd got him hymn books. And who should I get a parcel from but the wife of the Bishop of Vancouver, one parcel a month. The parcels contained jam, tea and cocoa, and for Canadian troops, coffee, and maybe a little jar of butter and cookies and beef dripping. The boys used to jump for joy when they saw a little jar of dripping come up in some of my parcels.

We were allowed to write one letter a month, full name, regimental unit, everything. We also were allowed to send one printed card every two weeks. You wrote your own name on the card, which had printed on it sentences like, "I have been in hospital," or "I am in hospital," "I expect to be in hospital", "I am well," "I am quite well," "Don't worry, all is well." You just ticked them off if they applied. But no man if he had any brains would tell his people in England if he had been in hospital or if he was going to hospital. You always painted the picture in proper colour. I always thought that my parents had plenty to bear anyway.

When I got back into the camp at the end of July Champion had been writing out by hand a couple of sheets of paper that the Germans had allowed him to send through their own channels to almost every camp in Germany, two pages of written quotes from the scriptures and old hymns, anything to build up the spirit of those who were ready to fall. I hadn't been back in camp a month before he said, "Fred, can you use a typewritter?" and I said, "I sure can." By this time I was the guy that was adopted for all the penmanship.

I was on top of the heap by this time. My feelings were that I had a bigger job to do more than ever. I had that inbred determination that I wasn't going to die in Germany, I knew I would get out some day.

Champion said to me "I'm going to try Diebel (the interpreter) I'm going to put him to the test. I'm going to tell him that he can have all the cigarettes that we can collect if he'll try to get us a secondhand typewriter." So in comes an old typewriter, an old Fox. It didn't take long before he said, "How about you writing a piece now? We are going to turn this scrap paper into a magazine." He was a marvellous fellow, very innovative. He said, "I'm going to get some of the boys in the camp who are fond of sketching." It was surprising some of the talent that was available. Anyway, the outcome of all this was that within three months Champion and I had the *Munster Church Times* in print. It was handled through German channels and it had been authorized. The Anglican Church in Lon-

don sent us hymn books and music, and we had male
quartets, male choruses, duets, soloists.

In August a neutral medical commission came in and
we'd just got this working beautifully. Even a German pastor
came in once a month to speak to the men. He would start
service each Sunday morning with the same line: "Let us
sing a Holy, Holy, Holy."

Anyway, this Swiss medical commission went through
every camp in Germany. It was late August 1916. They left
lists with the Germans of men who had been put on parade
and I was one who had been through the mill. There
weren't many who had refused to work. But I think I had
a constitution that was able to stand up when it was needed. I had lived a clean life. I hadn't been the goody-goody
type, mind you, but I had kept myself clean always. I was
called up for examination and I learned a bit later through
Diebel that they had recommended that I be interned
elsewhere with other men who had been designated for
the simple reason that we were of no further military use
to our country.

We heard nothing more of this until August 16th, 1918.
On that date the list of names came out for each block.
I was one of ninety men in Block Two out of about eight
thousand men and I might have been the only man with
two arms, two legs and two eyes. They lined us up quickly; I never had a chance to say good-bye to the others. All
I had time to do was collect my personal things, my watch
for instance, that I had kept throughout and a lot of notes
that I had made as I went, sewn into my jacket. They loaded us on the train and we went on through the Dutch
border, crossing it at Aachen on August 17th, my birthday.
They put us onto a vessel at Rotterdam called the
Glen Castle. Winston Churchill was on the ship and orders
were passed around that the bar would be open and the
boys fed. "Give them the best," he said.

We all got back to England and were dispersed to different hospitals in London. I was sent to King George

Hospital at Stafford Street Bridge where I was kept in quarantine for a few days. In the meantime they had either phoned or wired my mother that I was in the King George Hospital and that she could come down at her convenience. So mother, and my girl, came to visit me in the hospital, staying at the Union Jack Hotel nearby. Shortly afterwards I was advised that I would be given sixty days leave with full rations and full pay. I was married on October 8th at Hednesford in England. When I got home they put me on the scale and I weighed exactly eighty-nine pounds from my one hundred and forty.

On Armistice Day 1918 when I returned to camp at Barewood in England I remarked to my girl, my wife, "I will most likely be coming home for Christmas." On December 8th they moved us to Liverpool by train and onto a forty-five hundred ton hospital ship. We sailed on December 9th and had a very nice trip.

We eventually arrived in Calgary on Christmas morning. There were hundreds of women there with fruit and cigarettes. A couple of days later we reached Vancouver and were sent to Shaughnessy hospital. I was in Shaughnessy for several months. One morning my picture was in the *Vancouver Sun* with a story about where I'd been and what had happened. A man alongside of whom I had laid in the POW hospital came up to see me. He had been repatriated sooner than I. He had married and his wife was a nurse in the hospital. She'd lost her first husband in the merchant navy; he had been skipper on one of the smaller vessels that had been sunk by the Germans. When I got my discharge on June 12, 1919, I went to live with them for a short time. The next day after my discharge I went to report to the CPR for duty. They didn't have anything at the time but they called me later and I worked my first shift, the graveyard shift at Vancouver Exhibition.

So that was it. My shot at the Kaiser's War.

24

Athabaskans

Len Burrow and Emile Beaudoin

In the early hours of the morning of April 29th, 1944 the *Athabaskan* survivors were wearily resisting the cold water of the English Channel, wondering what was going to happen in the next hour or so. The desolate calm was suddenly broken by shouts: "Look — over there!" All eyes turned to the south, where three dark objects were growing steadily larger. As they closed on the *Athabaskan* it became evident that they were enemy ships. The larger one proved to be an Elbing class destroyer, T-24, which but a few hours before had been battling against *Athabaskan* and her sister-ship *Haida*. Now, she was on a mission of mercy.

When all possible survivors had been taken aboard the rescue ships they were brought to Brest, where the more badly injured prisoners were laid on stretchers, placed in ambulances, and taken to a hospital. When one of the survivors came to, he recalled he "was in paper bandages, my head was shaved and a ring had been sawed off my finger." As the remainder prepared to board trucks, the Free French Maquis fired three shots at the Germans. One bullet ricocheted off the pavement in front of the trucks, but no one was hit. The German guards did not fire back, but they got the vehicles moving out of the area as quickly as possible. The prisoners were taken to a four-storey building occupied by the Kriegsmarine, and which was formerly a girl's school, called Couvent Sainte Louise.

As they entered the quadrangle of the convent the uninvited guests were immediately surrounded by guards with rifles and machine-guns. Looking up they saw in a doorway about a dozen German ratings. From their wounds and from the gloating expressions on their faces, the Athabaskans surmised that they were the survivors of the Elbing destroyer T-29 they had sunk three days previously. This was confirmed later, as well as the fact that some of their guards were survivors from the Elbing destroyer T-27, another one of *Athabaskan's* former foes.

Orders in German meant nothing to the Canadian sailors, and it was the beckoning and the prods of rifle barrels which finally persuaded them to move inside the building. Here they showered with hot water; the German-manufactured soap was useless for lathering but they managed to clean up. Then they were issued with French Navy jumpers and trousers and German sports shoes and directed to one end of a gymnasium where three rows of straw-filled mattresses were laid out on the floor for them to rest on. At least eight German naval ratings, with tommy-guns at the ready, faced the Canadians. Conversation was forbidden and it was only when they lined up to go to the toilet that they were able to communicate. A blanket was issued to each man which was inadequate to combat the cool damp air, but sheer exhaustion finally brought refreshing sleep.

Dawn on Sunday, April 30th broke with the guards shaking all prisoners awake. They were given towels and soap for washing in cold water. Later, a slice of dark bread, jam and *ersatz* coffee was brought to them. They were left pretty much on their own for the day, but with the armed guards still on duty. Sunday dinner consisted of bread and a soupy mess of sweet macaroni which satisfied their hunger temporarily. Supper was a repeat of breakfast. The following day, the interrogations began. The Athabaskans were questioned one at a time. With the aid of cigarettes and schnapps as tempting bait and in devious subtle ways, the interrogation team attempted to ferret out information about the ship and her equipment, but all the enemy got was name, rating and official number. Asdic, radar and wireless operators received extra special attention from the inquisitors because of their technical knowledge in those important branches. The interrogators processed about four men per hour.

During that time they stayed in Brest, some of the survivors were taken by the Germans to the neighbouring seacoast to identify bodies which had been washed ashore. These were buried in the town.

On Thursday the 4th of May the Athabaskans were ordered to get ready to leave for an unknown destination. One group was marched to the rear of the convent and ordered to face a high concrete wall. They were told to stand at attention while six guards stood behind them, constantly cocking their rifles. "This is it," thought the trembling seamen. After about twenty minutes of this torture, the guards ordered them into a truck, waiting to go to the railway station.

On Saturday May 6th their train passed through Nantes, Orleans and Troyes. At sunset it took them through Ars/Mosel and Metz. It was now D-Day minus 30 and within a month the Allies would be landing on the coast of Normandy. The Athabaskans had witnessed some of the preparations for this giant assault and although they did not know its exact date, they surmised it would happen in the not-too-distant future. Their long, tedious journey brought them to Bremen, and eventually Marlag and Milag Nord, a POW camp for captured Allied naval and merchant seamen.

When *Athabaskan* came into service in 1943, only four

of an original sixteen British Tribals remained afloat. *Athabaskan's* career, unhappily, was to follow the pattern of so many of her illustrious sisters. In a short life of fifteen months, of which three were spent licking her wounds, she was pounded by the sea and battered by bombs, gunfire and torpedoes.

*   *   *   *

Len Burrow and his wife Jessica sat down on the rocky French seashore of the English Channel on a sunny day in April 1973. They had just completed the personal pilgrimage part of a European tour which had taken them through Germany, Holland, Belgium and France. And now they were discussing many aspects of the past few days which had proven exceedingly stirring for them. Many battle sites of both world wars had been visited along with tours through adjacent war cemeteries. It had been a memorable journey because each pilgrim had more than a passing interest in the historic panorama. Both had had fathers who had faithfully served as citizen soldiers in World War I and each had lost their youngest brother in World War II. Consequently, a generation after the second conflict, the weary travellers had returned to pay homage to Canada's dead. At Plouescat, they had gone to the communal cemetery where tribute was paid to the fifty-nine known and unknown members of *Athabaskan's* crew who are buried there. A Canadian dime was placed beside one of the stone markers inscribed to an unknown sailor. For conceivably, they thought, it could be the resting place of Leading Seaman William O. Burrow whose whereabouts was unknown. The young sailor had been posted as missing, along with many of his shipmates after the sinking of their ship, and not a single clue nor trace of him had surfaced in nearly thirty years. Official records had listed him — missing presumed dead.

Suddenly, they remembered that the Secretary-General

of Plouescat had mentioned the name of a former crew member who had passed through a year before on his way to a Naval Veterans' convention in Germany. His name was Beaudoin and he lived in Sainte Foy, Quebec — perhaps this man could be of some help and assistance. The stranger was contacted during the following summer and he proved to be the missing first link in the long chain of events and activities which undergird this naval drama.

Emile Beaudoin joined the RCNVR in 1940, graduating later as a telegraphist. He was aboard the Corvette HMCS *Levis* when she was torpedoed in the North Atlantic off Iceland in September 1941, so he was well aware of the perils of the deep. He was a crew member of *Athabaskan* when she made her last patrol; luckily he was rescued by the enemy and was forced to spend a year as a prisoner-of-war.

When Lieutenant-Commander John H. Stubbs, DSO, RCN, assumed command of *Athabaskan* on November 6th, 1943, he found to his dismay that he had inherited a commander's nightmare — an unhappy ship. He could sense an uneasy spirit prevailing throughout the ship. In fact, everybody seemed to want to get away from it all. Morale was at a low ebb; many members of the ship's company were under punishment and a great number of men were putting in for draft to take courses. This general feeling could thus be explained:

Superstition among seamen is as legendary as their colorful vocabulary, which comes in varying shades of blue. Omens and signs of bad luck have been dogging the heels of every naval disaster, from the *Titanic* on down. *Athabaskan* was no exception. As a matter of fact, the men felt that the ship was jinxed, having taken more than her share of knocks. She had been constantly in trouble: bombed while under construction; her bow damaged alongside an oiler, her hull strained by heavy weather. She had had a collision with a gate vessel. On the Russian convoy, were it not for a leaking condenser, she would have been present at the sinking of the *Scharnhorst*. In addition she was the first warship to have been hit by a new type of glider bomb.

Her new captain was quick to notice that the men did not appear to smile, laugh or sing; a complete change from his tour of duty with *Assiniboine*. Calling a meeting of officers in the wardroom, he proceeded to mention his observations and told them that there had to be a strong team-spirit between all ranks if *Athabaskan* were to become a first-class fighting ship. He went on to say that he could get along fine without officers, but that he needed the men who would run the ship for him. With this gentle threat, he admonished them to get on the job without delay.

Stubbs then asked the boatswain to pipe the order: "Clear lower decks!" All seamen not on duty assembled at the waist of the ship where he gave them a short pep talk. By the time he had finished speaking, the morale had gone up tremendously.

On the second night after Stubbs had assumed command, Able Seaman Don Newman was on duty as Quartermaster's Messenger. He was approached by Sub-Lieutenant Robert Annett with a message from the captain, requesting a set of poker dice. Annett and Newman proceeded to the seamen's mess, where the officer discreetly inquired if any dice were available. Eventually a set was produced. Annett signed a chit for them and quickly returned to the Wardroom. Since gambling of any kind was forbidden in RCN ships, Stubbs' gesture became another morale booster.

On another occasion, Stubbs came across one of his officers berating some seamen who were working alongside the ship at the boring task of chipping and painting. Apparently the work was not to the officer's satisfaction and he was letting them know in salty naval language. The interested captain quietly suggested to the officer that perhaps he should don overalls, slide over the side and show the men just how the job should be done.

In an effort to relieve the strain of continuous patrols

along the enemy-held coast, Stubbs organized parties and receptions aboard ship whenever the demanding schedule of Channel activity allowed. Plymouth people were invited aboard on several occasions, and some lasting relationships developed as a result. Some Athabaskans met girls and became good friends, while others fell in love with local girls and were subsequently married.

Back in harbour after a night patrol, Stubbs displayed his typical "no-nonsense" approach to the business of war. *Athabaskan* entered Devonport Dock at daybreak and steered to come along the starboard side of HMCS *Prince Robert*. There was no duty watch to receive *Athabaskan's* lines, so Stubbs conned his ship's bow in so that some of his men could jump aboard the *Robert* and tie up. Her captain, on deck for his morning constitutional, stopped dead in his tracks and bellowed out to *Athabaskan's* bridge: "Get those men out of the rig of the day off my ship." Taken aback but unperturbed by this rude welcome, Stubbs retorted loud and clear, "Sir, my men are tired and hungry. They have been standing to action stations all night. Where is your duty watch to receive our lines? This is a fighting ship — not a banana boat, like yours!"

This "let's get on with the job" attitude was typical of all Canadian servicemen and was the spirit which spurred them on to victory. Spit and polish was necessary to a certain degree, they admitted, and perhaps there were some finer points involved, but there was a war to be won and it could not be done in Number Ones.

25

Auschwitz

Doug Bennett

from a taped interview

I was taken prisoner at Dieppe in 1942 and, as we were going through our prison camps, they picked the medics to go to Auschwitz. There were about three hundred of us.

We didn't know what the smell was. The prisoners-of-war who were sent there were to lay pipes. It wasn't until we got back that we learned what it was all about — people burning in the furnaces and all the gas going on. We were laying pipes and the idea under the Geneva Convention was that we were only allowed to take those pipes within thirty feet of the building and then the Germans would have to continue. Our boys put great big stones in the middle of the pipes and I'm sure glad I was not there when that thing went up, because it must have taken half the camp with it.

Then they found out that we were a bunch of Canadians and they got a little excited about it and one morning we woke up and there were tanks and machine-gun posts all around the camps, and the Kommandant came out and he said, "Now, look, there's going to be a lot of death here. You either do what we want you to do or —." But two weeks after that, they packed it in and sent us back because they were getting a little scared.

We hadn't seen masses of people lining up to get gassed. We were on the side, nowhere near the railroad depot where these people were coming in — on the other side of the furnaces and whatever they were doing. We could see the smoke. But we didn't know at the time what was going on. We thought we were probably working on a munitions thing. However, there was one time when the fellows were digging ditches and there was a German political prisoner-of-war who was working and he had to "go". The German guard looked at him and said, "You're working." And he said, "But I have to go."

And he went to make the move and the guard shot him.

26
Air Demonstration

Ray Smith

Stalag IVB was located on the sandy plains of East Saxony, near Muhlberg-Elbe, approximately ten kilometers south of Lonnewitz airfield, a Luftwaffe training base. The winter of 1943-44 was harsh for the prisoners-of-war confined there, and only the more hardy ventured outdoors for daily routine walks in the compound. Many hibernated from the frigid cold, seeking warmth in the uncomfortable confines of their bunks.

In late April, 1944, came the welcome arrival of spring, with its thawing snow and ice and, most importantly, warm sunshine.

It also brought low flying aircraft from Lonnewitz airfield buzzing our camp. The pilots apparently had discovered that one of our compounds consisted of RAF aircrew personnel, to whom they demonstrated their low-flying prowess. One warm, sunny afternoon the compound was filled with strolling prisoners, fresh from hibernation to take in the first really warm day of spring.

The Luftwaffe pilots took this opportunity for a low-flying demonstration over our compound, while the prisoners on the ground encouraged them to fly lower and lower in the hope of seeing one of them crash — not anticipating the tragedy that was to follow.

One Luftwaffe pilot, flying a JU 88, diving in too steep, too low and too fast, just missed the stilted guard-shack with his starboard wing, and mushed into the compound. With a surge of power he managed to be airborne again in an almost vertical climb, trailing a large section of barbed wire fencing behind him, and was seen to make a safe landing back at base.

But tragedy had struck. Two Canadian pilots, walking together, were struck by the JU 88. One had his leg shattered by the tailplane, while the other was slashed by the airscrews and died instantly. After having provoked the Lonnewitz pilots to fly lower and lower, we then complained bitterly to the camp Kommandant, which gave us an opportunity to start and win an argument.

It was ironical that a Canadian, who had survived several years as a prisoner-of-war, should then die in such a freak accident. The Kommandant granted a full military funeral at Neuburgsdorf cemetery, where some four thousand seven hundred prisoners-of-war lie buried. This concession was not afforded to many prisoners-of-war, of all nationalities, buried there. Later we were to learn that the Luftwaffe pilot was stripped of all rank, imprisoned, and thereafter sent to the Russian front as an infantry private, for having damaged one of "Der Fuhrer's" aircraft.

27

The Prisoner Of War

by Kenneth N. Laing
*(from a wartime log written while he was
confined at Stalag 383, Hohenfels, Bavaria)*

The Prisoner of war is a strangely pathetic figure — a youth conscious of no crime, yet deprived in the full vigour of his youth of his manhood, of nearly all the ordinary outlets of human activity; a soldier without the stimulus of active service or the sustaining consciousness of success or achievment; an exile living in an atmosphere of constant hostility; owing his very life to the sufferance of his captors; a man without rights.

Though living, he is dead, and dead with little glory. To his captors he is simply an additional embarrassment, another mouth to be fed, another body to be clothed. To his guards he is the most monotonous and hated of duties; and to the civilian population, he is the enemy in their power and without means of retaliation.

Among the prisoners there developed a distinct pathological condition, pathological in its nature to a varying degree. Herded together as they were in forced confinement without normal occupation, believing themselves hated and ill-treated, tortured in their uselessness in the hour of their country's need and by anxiety regarding their own people at home, alternating between hope and despair until their numbed hearts could feel no more, fighting without adequate encouragement against approaching lethargy, with the blight of futility on all that they did — it is little wonder that so many of them sank into a malaise that has been called "Barbed Wire Disease".

The barbed wire was ever present to the prisoner. From morning to night, from day to day, throughout the interminable weary months and years it was there. Through it he gained tantalizing glimpses of the great free world beyond; by it he was forever hurled back into his own drab and hated camp. The barbed wire shut him out from the world of activity and satisfaction. It also shut him in with the herd of fellow-prisoners. There was no privacy, no solitude in a prison camp. The inevitable result of this indiscriminate and unmitigated herding was an intense irritability, a growing hatred of fellow prisoners and a confirmed habit of suspicion.

The captive fresh from his experiences at the front, rejoicing in his safety, at first threw himself with ardour into all the camp activities. But the final effect of prison life was a tendency by the captive to withdraw into himself in a surly ill-humour.

To the experience of many, fate added another horror — ill health. For those who were really sick there were hospitals, but for those with shattered nerves and ordinary disabilities of life that create misery without disability, there could be no relief. Conditions of crowding, undernourishment and exposure imposed the most exquisite torture on the unfit.

Depression tended always to add to the problems of this unfortunate group. Epidemic diseases were not unknown in the camps and one can hardly imagine circumstances less favourable for a contest with infection.

Pen and ink drawing in a kriegie's diary by J. Westmacott.

The dark side of the picture has been presented but we do not wish to give the exaggerated impression that all the prisoners succumbed to their fate. One could not have been surprised if they had done so, but the real wonder is that so many struggled so valiantly to preserve their manhood and to keep their interest alive.

In every camp there were heroes who resisted depression and put forth every effort to save themselves and their comrades. It was an inglorious and for the most part a thankless task. Courage and resourcefulness of the highest order were required and constant watchfulness alone could save what courage and resourcefulness set up.

There were men who were the cornerstones of these organizations that grew up within the camps expressing in concrete terms the deliberate attempts of men to help themselves in a desperate situation. Religiously-minded men impelled by the inspiration of their inner convictions made superhuman efforts to spread the Christian spirit of hope and friendliness among their discouraged comrades. It was not a bad place in which to test the reality of religious faith.

In the question of food, the prisoners lacked not only the frills of diet but the very essentials. The warring coun-

Bringing in the soup ration. Soup was most often made with cabbage or millet.

This still was made out of Klim tins and tubing probably stolen or traded from German guards.

tries lacked an adequate supply of fats, of sugars and other prime elements; therefore, the prisoners of war suffered not only from the monotony of diet but from its actual inadequacy. The first requirement of the prisoner of war was food. Without supplementary rations, health and strength could not have been maintained.

The other needs were quite as real, however. At this point we encounter another contrast between the conditions of the prisoner and the fighting man. The prison camps were full of idle men. There was no dearth of workers. Prisoners of war were, as a rule, eager to help themselves. Their lack was equipment. With the best will in the world, work cannot be carried on without material. The welfare problem was to stimulate activity and provide the material and equipment necessary.

The width of infinity separated the possession of even a little work from having nothing at all. When it is remembered what these idle men lacked, the spiritual value of material equipment may be better comprehended. Books, stationery, musical instruments, educational text books, gramaphones, games, Bible and hymn sheets, these cannot be created in prison camps; but what is idle life like month after month without them?

The small working camps were not troubled with the difficulty of finding employment but the hours of leisure were blank; to them games, books and the like were godsends indeed. Here and there in the prison camps a triumphant conception took possession of leaders among the imprisoned men. With reasonable help from the outside it appeared life might be made bearable. It did not seem a remote possibility that some pleasure and at least a degree of contentment might be wrested from the hands of hard fate. The achievement of this second of mental progress opened up a new vista as some men saw the period of internment could be made a time of growth and personal improvement.

The opportunity of the prison camps, that was the thing.

The "dhobie stick" — Washing clothes is not easy in prison camp but a Klim tin on the end of a stick helps a great deal.

With the establishment of lecture courses, educational classes, dramatic clubs, athletics and regular religious services there appeared in certain camps a well-organized social life; and not a few men came out of the experience better than they were when they entered it.

Such an achievement must be regarded as an outstanding triumph of the human spirit.

28

Jack Rabbit

Ray Heard

Jack was a rabbit breeder. He had managed to secure a couple early in 1941, when he was in the camp at Thorn in Poland. In those days a rabbit in the pot was better than a Red Cross parcel tossing on a hostile ocean somewhere between Halifax and Marseilles. When Jack took up rabbit breeding, his hut was never short of meat.

On being transferred from Thorn to another Stalag, Jack had to meet the problem of transporting his buck and doe. The Germans refused to consider them Jack's legitimate chattels so, true to the POW's ability to adapt himself to changed circumstances, he was forced to circumvent the Kommandant's ruling. Having consulted the bandmaster, he contrived to smuggle them inside a bass drum.

As the period of our enforced detention in the Third Reich lengthened, so the purely materialistic need for proteins changed George's attitude and affection for living things, in this case towards his rabbits.

One day a hutmate whose duty was to feed his charges omitted to fasten the hutch door securely. Jack went to the hutch a few minutes later and noticed that his precious buck, the one that had sired many a tasty meal, had fled.

He called at neighbouring huts, urgently asking for news of the escape. He began an intensive search and eventually discovered that the buck had last been seen making for the wire fence near one of the guard towers.

In single-minded pursuit Jack ignored the Kommandant's warning that any prisoner-of-war who crossed the trip wire did so at his own risk.

Espying his rabbit, he leapt over the dividing trip-wire into the forbidden area separating the main wire barrier from the camp.

By now the sentry in the tower had his rifle up to his shoulder and was taking aim. Our terrified shouts were too late for Jack. Two shots struck him squarely in the chest and he fell, without an angry word but with a gasp which brought him back to reality.

Some of us were about to cross the trip-wire to help him, but the sentry waved us back, his rifle pointing in our direction.

The rabbit jumped from Jack's weakening hands and, ironically, ran back into the camp. Clawing his way back to the trip-wire, Jack managed to get close enough for us to drag him away and bear him to the nearest hut.

The sentry lowered his rifle, calmly went to the telephone and said something into it. He had fulfilled his instructions. Jack was in the wrong. These facts the Kommandant told our "Man of Confidence" later. The Kommandant genuinely regretted the "incident" — but he pointed out that we had to realize that millions were dying on the Russian Front, in France, the Low Countries, Germany and the Far East at that time. We couldn't really expect him to be too impressed by the death of an enemy soldier who was shot chasing a rabbit. The guard had a job to do, he argued, just as had the aircrews who didn't know where their bombs were dropping when they attacked towns and villages.

Military funeral at POW cemetery.

29
Man's Inhumanity

Ed Carter-Edwards
from a taped interview

We had been bombing the 5th and 6th of June, 1944 and were slated to bomb June 7th, which would have been trip twenty-two. In relation to some of the other targets, it was relatively light — a marshalling yard outside Paris. We didn't anticipate too much flak, really no problem at all. Maybe the one thing against us was that we went in at a relatively low altitude, around sixteen thousand feet, and going into our target, we got hit by light anti-aircraft ground fire. It struck our aircraft on the port wing and set the whole wing on fire. The pilot tried to extinguish the flames, but unsuccessfully, and it became quite obvious we were in serious trouble. So he told us to abandon ship and we all bailed out. I went out the front end of the aircraft, jumped and rolled forward but the wind caught me and shipped me back. My chute opened, though I don't remember opening it. I guess I forgot to tighten my harness and when the chute opened, it gave me such a jolt it just about split me in half. I often joke that it's probably why I'm a tenor today.

It was 1:20 in the morning when we got hit, which made it the morning of the 8th. The aircraft was still airborne at this stage. It seemed to carry on a fairly straight course for a little, then it turned around and came back and it looked as if it was heading for us. I say "us" because I could see a couple of other chutes floating down by the light of the aircraft which, by then, was burning very strongly. It passed near us and then just sort of faltered and went down and crashed into the ground with a huge roar and flame. We could see a river, the Seine, and what looked like a church in the background and a little bit of a village. The burning plane was like a beacon, lighting up the whole sky and I noticed that there were seven other parachutes in the sky, which meant we were all safely out of the aircraft. There was also a fighter floating around at this time, a Focke-Wulf 190. He was so close I could almost touch him as he went by, but he didn't cause any harm and our main concern was trying to get down and get away from that area.

When we landed it was black, of course; we were in the dark area of the ground, couldn't in fact see where the ground was at this stage. We hit it pretty hard and gathered up our chutes. We were in a field and we ran away from the aircraft which we could hear and see burning in the distance, toward the edge of the field where we hid our chutes under some leaves and bushes. As I looked back towards the aircraft, I saw a shadow going by between the aircraft and myself and thought, "That could be one of our boys." So I hollered, "Who is it? It's Ed."

The voice replied, "It's Tom."

Tom was our bomb-aimer. We approached one another, offered congratulations on being alive, and proceeded to run. We came to a small wood where we stopped to gather our breath. Rather than run together, we decided one of us would run ahead of the other so if anybody came on us unexpectedly one could get away. Tom went ahead of me and we were hurrying through the bush, when all of a sudden lights came on to our right and there was the sound of loud voices. We started to run again. It was dark and we didn't know where we were going. Tom was so far ahead of me, I couldn't see him. I came to a fork in the path we were on, stopped and called out to him, although not loudly for fear of being heard by whoever was pursuing us, but loud enough so Tom could hear. There was no answer so I had to make up my mind which way Tom had taken, left or right. I took the path to the right. That was my mistake. I never saw him again until I got back home in 1945.

I carried on along the path and finally, totally exhausted, flopped down onto some bushes. During the course of the night it started to rain and, unknown to me, I was lying in a bed of nettles and woke up in the morning covered in red itchy sores, wet, cold, and miserable. I could hear church bells chiming in the distance so I knew I was fairly close to a town, so I stayed there all that day. By evening, I was desperate. I thought, "I've gotta make a move." So I got up, went toward the area where I'd heard the bells ringing and, sure enough, came to a town. I knocked on the door of a house. The first couple of times nobody answered. The third time, a man came to the door. I told him I was a Canadian airman and wanted help. He slammed the door in my face, an incident repeated with the next few houses.

Finally, I came to a place with a high wall in front of it. As I walked by the wall I could hear voices behind it. I continued walking to a gate in the wall where I saw the owners of the voices. I started to speak to them and a lady said to me in plain English, "Who are you? What do you want?"

I replied that I was a Canadian airman who had been shot down a couple of nights ago and that I was hungry and would they give me something to eat. They took me into the house and gave me bread and milk but, justifiably, they wouldn't allow me to stay. After they had listened to

my story, they took me across the road to an old barn. I
stayed there during the daytime and, at night, they would
come over and get me and bring me back to the house and
give me some more food. Then I would go back to the barn.
This went on for a week, then, finally, the lady told me
the Gestapo were in the area and were aware that there
was an airman in hiding and that I would have to leave.
They made arrangements for someone from the French
Underground to come and get me. I was taken to another
house. I had got rid of my uniform and was given pants,
jacket, a beret, a haversack, and a bicycle. I was taken by
bike to a house in a wood quite a way away. The place
was owned by a widow there, whose husband had fought
with the French and been killed.

After a week, I got a visit from the French Underground,
a man and a woman from Paris. To prove I was who I said
I was, I gave them my papers and identity photographs.
A couple of days later they came back with false papers
signed by the Gestapo and covered with swastikas, with
my name changed to "Edward Cartier," a "jeweller's
helper" who had been sent to the country "for his health".
I was told I would be taken to Paris. They tried to get all
the Allied airmen on the run to Paris where they would
usually be shipped to Spain.

A few days later I was fetched by the couple. We travelled by bicycle and via rowboat across the Seine and, eventually, got on board a train where, for the first time since
being shot down, I had the alarming experience of coming face to face with a German soldier. He was on guard
at the door and to my eyes seemed about four hundred
pounds in weight and eight feet in height, with shoulders
on him eight feet wide. He had an automatic machine-gun
cradled in his arms and "potato-mashers" stuck in his belt
and jackboots.

The couple who were with me warned me not to look
at anybody on the train and to pretend to be sleeping. One
sat beside and one sat opposite me. The one opposite kept

kicking me and motioning me to go to sleep. After several hours we arrived in Paris where I was given instructions that, if by chance any trouble arose or if we got stopped for an identity-check, my companions would try to create a distraction so I could get away. But luckily we got through the check and everything was okay. We went to an apartment where we stayed a few hours before I was transferred to another apartment. I was there about three days, told not to answer the door to anybody unless I got a certain knock. In the meantime, I had no food, no water, nothing. After that time I was getting desperate, when, at last, I heard the knock. There was a big fellow standing there. He said his name was George and he was with the French Underground — a big, heavy-set guy, wearing dark-rimmed glasses. He told me he was going to take me to Spain by car and that some of my Allied airmen were downstairs waiting for me. So I went with him and sure enough, there were three other Allied airmen in the car, a Mercedes. We introduced ourselves, all, of course, glad to meet one another. They had been given the same story and under the same set of circumstances, i.e. we were all suppose to go to Spain by car.

But as it happened, this fellow was a collaborator, and instead of taking us to Spain by car, he drove us to the outskirts near a prison called Fresnes, and turned us over to a German outpost. He just drove up to them, stopped the car, got out and went over to them. Then a horde of Germans came over, yanked the car door open and dragged us out, putting the boot to us and the rifle. They really roughed us up. Finally, I stood up to this one German officer who came up to me, whipping out a big Luger and jabbing it in my face. He said, "British?"

I said, "No. Canadian." He went on jabbing, forcing me to the ground. I got up again. He grabbed my dog tags which I had retained, threw them on the ground and snarled, "Now who are you and what are you? Prove yourself."

We were thrown into a German lorry and taken to

Fresnes prison, a civilian jail, primarily for political prisoners, members of the Underground and blackmarketeers. We were there about six weeks. During the first week we were constantly taken down to the head office and interrogated, threatened that we would be shot if we didn't give them information. We were really given a rough time, but once they realized that we weren't going to tell them anything except rank, name and number, they didn't bother us anymore.

There were four of us in a little cell about six feet by eight. We slept on straw mattresses and the food was terrible. Very little food, very little sanitation. The place was lousy with lice and fleas and it got to a point, after about six weeks, when we became awfully sick, dizzy when we stood up, light-headed and suffering dysentery. Some of us were starting to pass blood.

By this time, the Allies were getting close to Paris. We could hear the artillery and the bombing was becoming increasingly intense. So one day it was decided to evacuate the whole prison. They took everybody out and down to the inner courtyard. I saw the couple that had been instrumental in hiding me while I was with the Underground. Obviously they had been turned in by someone. My heart just swelled right up. Words cannot express my feelings when I realized they had been tricked and were facing maybe the same thing I was facing or even worse, death. I was terribly upset because they were there probably because of me and maybe some others like me. What a terrible price to pay.

We were whipped over to the marshalling yards and jammed into French boxcars, the old "forty hommes, eight chevaux". They didn't obey that rule. The car we were in in contained seventy or eighty, jammed in so bad you couldn't even sit. We were in it about a week, not knowing where we were heading. During the course of the week we were strafed by our allies and had very little food or sanitation. In fact, sanitation consisted of a big open bucket in the middle of the boxcar, not very pleasant for those who were in the centre, close to the pail because the cars were not very stable. They would jiggle and the people in the centre were constantly being saturated.

Once we got hung up in a tunnel. The Allies had bombed the other end, and the train was trapped. It seemed like years we were in there but was probably only a few hours. The place was black, the stench of the engines choking. There were several thousand people involved in the convoy, men, women, kids. There was constant screaming and crying, and constant threats by the Germans to machine-gun the cars. The air was foul; we were getting to the point where we were becoming asphyxiated.

After what seemed like an eternity, the train started to back out. The Germans asked for six volunteers and six of our men stepped forward. They said, "Okay, fine. The rest of the Allied airmen will carry the contents of the train to the other side of the bombed area and, if anybody escapes, these six will be executed." So there was no possible way to escape with six of our people being held as hostages.

Finally we got the thing moving again and, after several more days of constant threats of being shot, bombarded, grenaded and everything, we finally arrived at this place. As soon as we got there we knew something was wrong. Men in light green jackets came along the train, opened the doors and proceeded to boot and rifle-butt everybody out of the cars. Of course, we couldn't understand what they were saying and they showed no mercy to anyone. We were herded into the camp.

At this time the name Buchenwald didn't mean anything to us, but as soon as we got in we realized that we were in a place that wasn't very hospitable. The first people to meet us were prisoners who said, "American nix good." That really put the fear of God in us. As we walked to the lower compound and saw what was around us we realized this was a terrible place; people starving, walking skeletons, the ground just stone and dirt and no shelter —

and the guards, dogs, and high barbed-wire electric fence
— everything gave you a sense of foreboding.

All the newcomers to the lower compound were placed in an area that was wired off and which was just cob-
blestone. We were just left — that was it — we just stayed
there with what we had. We slept with no blankets and
very little food. It was just like sleeping out in a corral. No
trees, no buildings — nothing — like sleeping on a cob-
blestone road.

We were in this area for about three weeks. While we
were there they took all our clothes and gave us each a
shirt and a pair of pants from the camp. Then they cut off
all our hair, every strand from all parts of our bodies. The
guys who sheared us were Russian prisoners from the camp,
which held around forty thousand people. There were Russians, Poles, Czechs, French, every nationality imaginable;
political prisoners, soldiers, black market agents, and
everything else. The fellows who clipped us were most
unkind. They used old-type clippers, cutting underneath
our arms and between our legs. They were so rough they
nicked us pretty badly; we were bleeding all over and to
finish off their pleasure, they used a swab and stuck it in
a pail of fluid and dipped it under our arms and between
our legs. It was some kind of lye solution and oh, did it
burn. Imagine one hundred and seventy Allied airmen dan-
cing around like stripped chickens. That was the one and
only time we ever did laugh. It was funny but painful at
the same time.

While we were in the lower compound, around the
first part of September, the Americans came over and bombed a factory on the outskirts of the town where they built
parts of the V-1 and V-2 rockets. About six thousand people from the camp worked in the factory and the Americans
got to hear about it. They came over on a beautiful, bright,
sunny day. We could hear aircraft in the distance and suddenly a white marker appeared right over our heads and
it wasn't too long before we could see a whole horde of

Flying Fortresses heading in our direction.

The resulting air-raid killed and crippled and maimed thousands of people. It created chaos in the camp, with people running in every direction, just total panic, and the Germans threatening to shoot us. They gathered all of us they could and took us to try and fight the fires, huge fires, within the camp. Some of the buildings had been hit and were on fire. We had no shoes. All we had on were pants. We had to try to put out the fires to the best of our ability.

When the thing was over, it was sad to hear that so many had been killed. But the bombers did a good job on the factory; they really wiped it out with the loss of life as low as possible.

After the bombing, we were taken to the head building. The Kommandant, Koch, was pretty upset. He threatened us with having to pay for the damage. While we were there, for some reason, we were all given needles in the chest. The needles contained some kind of sickly green fluid. I can't recall whether some of us had fainted or got sick but we were all given these needles in our chests. Shortly after we returned to the lower compound, I took sick with pneumonia and pleurisy. I was sent to another area where all the dead and dying were housed.

Some of the things I witnessed and experienced while in the lower compound were different from the average prisoner-of-war experience. When I say "average" I don't mean it lightly, because no prisoner-of-war experience should be treated lightly. But they were different in that we suffered starvation and witnessed beatings and shootings and people forced to behave like animals. For instance, when we first arrived we were given black bread. It was totally unpalatable to us and we threw the stuff on the ground. There would be forty, fifty guys jumping on it like a pack of wild dogs. We did this for a few days but after a while we suddenly realized that we would have to do something or we would starve to death. So we finally got to like it a little bit, or, at least, we ate it with the soup which was terrible, with fleas and lice and all kinds of bugs floating in it. The coffee was what they called *ersatz* — no cream or sugar, of course, just brown gook that was terrible to taste, but you couldn't drink the water because it would give you dysentery, so you had to drink this stuff. At least it had been boiled.

I had dysentery and was passing blood. Somehow we were able to burn the black bread to make toast out of it. I thought that by burning it, the carbon would help to prevent the dysentery.

When the Germans walked by you had to stand at attention, facing them with the palms of your hands by your sides. If you happened to stand in a natural position with a bit of a fist in your hand, you got a rifle in the face or a kick in the groin. It was total submission. You had to let them know they were the masters. If there was any doubt in their minds, they would strike out first.

When I was in the lower compound, we had roll-call which used to last for hours. With all the dysentery, a lot of people couldn't wait to go to the washroom; they had to do it right where they were standing. They had to drop their pants and lift up a stone and do it on the stone or do it right there on the ground. I remember one time when this one chap couldn't wait any longer, and as soon as the German guard had passed, he hurried over to the washroom, which was a hut. The guard came back before he came out and, as the guard came in one side and he came out the other, running, holding his pants up, the guard caught up with him, pulled out a revolver and shot him dead, right on the spot.

There was no mercy shown towards anybody by the Germans or by the group leaders. There were some prisoners who were privileged within the camp. They were big, husky sadists who always carried a big hunk of two-by-four about five feet long which they used with lots of strength, believe me. They were chosen for their "character" and they split heads and laid other inmates to the ground. For this policing of the camp, they received extra privileges. I witnessed many guys being beaten. You were unable to protect them or assist because you would end up the same way, so you had to stand by and see these things happen. It was demoralizing. This constant shattering of human dignity and this total disrespect for a fellow human-being is probably one of the elements that scarred my memory and that of many others who were in the camp. It has stayed with me all these years. Even today, I abhor disrespect by one person for another, whether it be a foreman to one of his workers, or a policeman to a pedestrian.

I feel that what was responsible for the mental breakdown of many of the people in these camps was the realization that there was no avenue of escape; no future; death by disease, death by starvation or being transported to work in the areas being bombed. It looked like no matter which way you turned, death faced you. While you were there and weren't actually working, you walked around aimlessly, viewing the experiences of the other human beings and the indignities they suffered. It was a landscape devoid of grass, trees, shrubs — no birds — nothing but suffering, starvation, diseased bodies all around you day and night. There was also the constant threat of being shot. Day or night, your life didn't matter one hoot. Then, too, there was the ever-present high electric fence, the barbed wire, the dogs, the guards, the machine guns, the total hopelessness of ever surviving. Death was everywhere.

I was told that before we got there, in the winter time, they used to take people — human people — human bodies, living bodies — and tie them, naked, to a tree or a stake and throw water on them until they were a frozen solid cake of ice. They used to stand out there for roll-call for hours in the snow. It was like Dante's *Inferno*, a terrible place to be. A lot of the stories that came out of the concentration camps will never be believed because peo-

ple can't believe that one human being could be so in-
humane towards another.

It's well-known that the Kommandant's wife, Ilse Koch,
the "Bitch of Buchenwald", had lamp-shades made out of
human skin. We were aware that this was going on. Apparently she would pick out some of the prisoners who had
beautiful tattoos on their bodies and she would have them
eliminated and the skin taken off and made into lamp-
shades.

The place was full of disease, every disease imaginable,
running rampant. The slightest little cut on your finger turned quickly into an ugly festering sore for which, of course,
there was no medication. You either survived or you didn't.
They did exterminate a lot of Jews, but Buchenwald was
basically a transfer camp for forced labour to go to bombed-
out areas. So there was quite a movement of people in and
out. Some stayed and worked in the factories but most of
them didn't stay too long. We couldn't speak the languages;
even those you could communicate with, with a little bit
of English, wouldn't be around very long.

The sewage was terrible. The toilet facilities were just
an open pit with a pole across the centre. If you had the
misfortune to fall off the pole into the hole, it was difficult
to find anybody to try to help you out. It was survival of
the fittest; you saved your energy for yourself and became
cruel and unkindly after a while. You almost became part
of the camp itself. It's unfortunate, but it just shows you
that the society we live in is very nice, but take away all
these things we are enjoying and it wouldn't take long for
people to revert to their savage ways. The lines are very,
very fine. Of course, this didn't happen in conventional
prisoner-of-war camps where things were totally different.
There, you did have some food and some humanity about
you. In this concentration camp, humanity wasn't prevalent
at all. It was, as I say, a sadistic survival of the fittest.

We Allied airmen did try to help one another because
of our training. We respected each other and we needed

each other. This was why we were able to survive. The other people in the camp only thought as individuals, thinking of themselves and not worried about the other guy. It's sad, but that's the way it was.

As for myself, I ended up with pneumonia and pleurisy, segregated from the rest of the guys and in the area with the dead and dying. I was delirious and out of my mind. As far as I know, I was in there from six to eight weeks. The only treatment I got was from one of the inmates, a professor from the University of Paris who was a doctor. He got hold of a syringe and planted it in my back, draining the fluid out of my lung. He did this at great risk to himself. He knew I was an Allied airman and he had sympathy for me and he tried to help me out. That's the only thing I ever had done for pneumonia and pleurisy. There was no medication, no aspirin, no antibiotics. You either lived or you died. If you survived, you were lucky; if you didn't, they used to take out dozens of bodies who had died during the night. They would pile them up on a homemade stretcher like cord-wood and carry them off to the crematorium. They were dying so fast, they couldn't burn them quick enough. They had some of the bodies stored in the shacks and sheds near the crematorium.

We had to sleep on a bit of straw mattress, no blankets or anything. Once in a while they would come through there with a hose and wash the whole place down — you and everything in it, even the bed where you were lying sick. It didn't make sense. There I was with pneumonia and pleurisy, and there they were soaking the whole bed and the whole place with water trying to wash it down. A lot of men who were lying there had dysentery, and, of course, the dysentery was running through the bed and onto the floors. The treatment and care was terrible. It was administered mainly by Russians and they didn't care whether you were clean or not. That didn't enter the picture at all. They had no mercy for anybody, even though they knew we were their allies. They didn't show any extra respect for us, none whatsoever. To them, we were just like the rest. I suppose they were concerned about their own survival.

It was this time in the shed that stands out most in my mind, probably because I was so close to death. Death was all around me; I saw it, I witnessed it, I heard it, I felt it — men crying out, gasping their last breath, calling out the names of their loved ones, kids, wives.

I was finally able to get out of the place. I wasn't out more than two days when I was forced to work on a railway line they were laying through the camp. I had to go and work up to my knees in mud, sick as I was. I complained to the guards but they just laughed at me and said that if I didn't like what I was doing, I could go visit the crematorium. That was the only sympathy I got. I realized again that my survival depended on my wits.

While we were working on the railway we dug an embankment. The Germans used to stand on top of it and kick stones and dirt down on us. It was wet and cold. They had dogs, and they used to gather the leash in their hands and then walk towards you and give a command and release the leash and the dog would jump for your face. It might get within an inch of your face, then they would pull back and have a big laugh. They thought this was a big joke.

Finally, I was able to contact a Dutch fellow named Kurt Barrs. Before he got picked up he had been working for the Dutch Underground. He had been training to be a doctor. Through some manipulation he was able to get my name taken off the workforce. He had me down as being dead. Put on a death sheet — I don't know how. He told me to keep out of sight as much as possible, which was kind of hard to do but there were so many people milling around you felt a bit more secure.

At this stage, I had been moved from the lower compound to the middle compound. The rest of the Allied airmen in Buchenwald had already been removed. Apparently the German airforce found out about us being there

It's quicker to shoot them than to starve them.

and they came down and removed us. There were stories that the Polish Underground working within Buchenwald got the message out to the German airforce and they came and took everybody out. But there were about ten of us who were sick (I can't remember who the others were) because, once I got into the middle compound, I was totally on my own. When I heard about the other fellows being gone, I believed I would never get out alive because I would be forgotten.

So there I was in this place until the end of November. We slept in terrible conditions on beds like bakers' shelves. They were about six feet wide, with four tiers of them against each wall, and people jammed in just like sardines. You couldn't move and, of course, there were no blankets or anything; you just slept in the clothes you had on your back. You never had a change of clothes. You had no toilet facilities, no washroom or soap.

I couldn't speak the language of the others around me.

I was totally lost. Luckily, through the grace of someone, toward the end of November, somebody from the German airforce came into the area and located me and took me out of there to a regular prisoner-of-war camp at Stalag 3. I still had on my pair of pants and my shirt and I had a pair of shoes by this time. The fellow who took me spoke excellent English. He was from New York City. Apparently he had been visiting Germany just before the war and got caught there when war was declared and had had to join up. I was in Stalag 3 for two and a half months when the Russians got too close to the camp. They were making a big push. The Germans decided to evacuate Stalag 3, which was at Sagan.

It was in December and January, 1945 when we were on the march. We slept in bombed-out factories and farmhouses. We finally ended up at Marlag and Milag N, a naval camp near Bremershaven. I was there until April 1st. When the Allies got close to camp, we were evacuated again, so, once more, we were on the road, marching east for about a month. During this time, we got shot at by our own fighters. We slept on the road or out in the fields. There was no covering at all.

Eventually, we were liberated near Lubeck in early May. We were immediately taken back behind the lines by the 2nd Cheshire Regiment and flown back to a German aerodrome. We were housed there for a couple of days, then flown back to England where we were deloused.

Finally I arrived back home in Hamilton, Ontario. After I got home, I still suffered the effects of Buchenwald and had to receive help at a convalescent hospital in Lancaster. I was there about three months and finally got straightened out and went back to work.

Luckily the years have cast some shadows over my mind, blacking out much of the Buchenwald experience. But the mental pictures remain, and are sometimes triggered easily by a war movie or if I hear a German accent, or even a siren or airplanes flying overhead. These things are not

"APPEL"

as bad as they used to be, but they are still there. I'm very happy to have survived but I still feel that it should never have happened. Not only that I shouldn't have suffered all these inhumanities and indignities, but also that for a nation, even a nation like Germany, it was totally wrong to develop these camps. What purpose did they serve, other than to cause suffering and indignity to human beings? I'm sure men and women deserve more than that, no matter what nationality they are and under what circumstances. These circumstances of degradation are totally unnecessary in the twentieth century. I'll never forget. It's the type of thing that will live with me and die with me.

I have great difficulty now in warming to any Germans; no matter how friendly they are or how far removed from the scene. They are still basically of that heritage; it's happened once, it's happened twice, and it could happen again — and this is one of the things I fear.

30

Christmas In Kriegieland

R. L. Masters

You want to know how we cooked when we were guests of the Third Reich? Well, I'll tell you. A good cook can turn out a fine dinner even in a kriegie (kriegsgefangener) camp, especially if he is a wizard at improvising. We had a combine of twenty men, and we pooled our resources. Monty (our room leader) was head man and chef, and the rest of us had jobs carrying water, sweeping floors and so on. We used a stove with tin can modifications.

Of course we pooled the food stuffs in our Red Cross Christmas parcels, and for a long time before Christmas Monty was busy baking cakes. He planned to have twenty individual cakes and one large communal.

Each Red Cross Christmas parcel contained a twelve-ounce can of turkey, one plum pudding, six ounces of stewed cherries, eight ounces of candy, eight ounces of cheese and some honey, and other Christmas sweets such as dates and nuts. To augment the supplies we swiped a few carrots for the bouillon cube consomme, and bought onions from the guards, in exchange for cigarettes, also enough rye flour to help a bit in the baking.

With this larder to draw from, Monty went to work on the large cake. He crushed Red Cross biscuits and mixed them with dry rye bread crumbs, margarine and Klim powdered milk, filled nine prune boxes with the mixture and baked them in the ashes. He built the nine cakes like a wall, with icing made from D bars for mortar.

For some time he had been saving prune stones; he roasted the kernels, ground them to powder with a stone, and mixed the powder with Klim, sugar and margarine. Honestly, you couldn't tell the result from marzipan. He spread a thick layer of this marzipan over his cake erection, and over that he put half an inch of D bar icing. D bars are emergency chocolate ration, with calcium and other concentrated values.

The individual cakes were made by a different method. Monty crumbled and dried the soft part of Deutsch rye bread . . . not the crusts, they tasted horrible . . . then mixed in margarine, raisins, chips of prunes, apricots and a little carrot, and flavored with roasted prune kernels and a touch of cinnamon. To make them rise he used soda bicarbonate tablets racketeered from the medical stores.

These cakes he baked in Klim tins, by placing three tins on the stove and inverting a pail over them. When they were baked he iced them with pink and white icing squeezed through a tube improvised from a Klim tin.

In addition to the Red cross puddings Monty made one of Deutsch bread with prunes, raisins and carrots. He filled a bowl, tied it in a cloth, put a stick through the knot, and suspended it in a pailful of boiling water for five hours. He invented a sauce of turnip jam, which is bright red, Klim and sugar heated together.

An hour before dinner Monty turned us out of the room while he set the tables. When we came in the tables were decorated with red and white crepe paper. At every man's place were a decorated cake, a new Red Cross face cloth

Christmas
1943

To Canadian Prisoners Of War

Our Christmas gift of two pounds of chocolate and three hundred cigarettes has been despatched to you and we trust will arrive safely and in good time. The thoughts of your friends and relations and of all your countrymen are with you this Christmas time. The message we send you is one of hope and faith. Hope that the New Year will bring a speedy end to the separation and hardships of war. Faith in the future that we will build together. May the coming year bring you back to us and restore peace to the peoples of the World.

A Happy Christmas and A Happier New Year

Beatrice Tobin Amelin

President

The Canadian Prisoners of War Relatives Association

. . . each a different color . . . and a place card. An American had drawn the cards, with a design of bells, and the initials of every Service represented in the combine:– RCAF, RAF, RNZAF, RAAF, USAAF, Paratroops.

We had to eat out of our kriegie bowls, and wash them between courses, but it wasn't much trouble, because the cooks had a good supply of hot water for that purpose. Here's the menu:

Consomme
Turkey with potato chips seasoned with onion
Plum pudding with Klim bash sauce
Stewed cherries
Christmas cake
Nuts, candy
Crackers and cheese

Tea   *Coffee*

The Swiss Y.M.C.A. had sent mild fireworks which went up with a whoosh and showered down flags and hats and tinsel.

Two Abwehr "goons", as we kriegies called the guards, came in an looked around. *"Das ist schon!"* one said quietly to the other.

We asked them about their celebration. They told us they each had a sausage about a yard long, and a loaf of bread. They said they put the sausages round their necks and danced around and had a fine time.

After dinner we had an orchestra consisting of a piano accordion, a saxophone and a clarinet. We sang, and "Hung the washing on the Siegfried Line" so often that it was a wonder the guards didn't come in and shut us down.

We were permitted to stay out in the compound if we wished until one o'clock, instead of coming in before sundown, as usual. The guards were posted thick around the lager, as an extra precaution. We went visiting, and kept open house ourselves. We set out biscuits with jam, cheese, honey, or a special confection, pineapple jam mixed with

All Canada joins
in
Warmest Christmas Greetings
and good wishes to you

W.L. Mackenzie King

1943   Prime Minister

cocoa, which has a unique flavour, really delicious.

As long as I live I'll never forget that Christmas dinner in a kriegie camp. I'll remember the nineteen other fellows in our combine, and Monty's wizardry with an improvised range. I do not think one of us will ever forget the Christmas parcels from the Red Cross.

31
Return To Eindhoven

Ray Silver
from a taped interview

I was shot down near Eindhoven, where Holland, Belgium and Germany come together. I landed in a grove, followed the usual procedure of removing anything that might be valuable to the enemy, burying it in the ground in the woods. This took about twenty minutes. Then I put on my flying pants and my battle dress trousers, covering the tops of my flying boots and removing my insignia, in order to look as civilian as possible.

Having walked for the next day and a half, I found myself, about eleven o'clock one morning, with my feet beginning to get sore and swollen from walking in flying boots. There had been a storm and, as I stopped to bale out my boots, I spotted a house that was sufficiently isolated, on a farm, that it minimized the chances of being seen by the Germans or collaborators.

I knocked on the door and a little blonde girl of about eleven appeared. I asked for her mother or father, words that are relatively universal. A Dutch farm woman came to the door, looked at me and immediately she could tell that I was bringing the smell of death to her doorstep.

I had kept the key to my room in the mess with "RAF" on it. I showed it to her. And this woman, a farmer's wife who had probably never in her entire life had to make a life-and-death decision, didn't hesitate one moment. To me it was one of the most remarkable performances I've ever seen in a human being. She just stepped back and without hesitating bowed me into her house. Late in the afternoon, her husband came home, found all the blinds drawn and me in there, and was most upset. A brother-in-law came over. Besides the eleven-year-old daughter, there was also a son, aged nine.

I was wringing wet from walking in the rain and they stripped me naked right beside the stove, until they could find some clothes. Not only did they outfit me completely in civilian gear, but the wife sewed all my escape kit into the seams of the clothes. The Dutch money went into the collar of a red silk peasant-type shirt and the maps went into the cuffs. Finally, she even sewed that little goddam hacksaw they used to put in there, the most incriminating thing, into the sweat band of the pants. She spotted the little compass from my escape kit and wanted it for a souvenir.

These people could only speak Flemish, so we conversed in sign language. Their house was only about one thousand feet from the Belgian border and they were trying to tell me that, if I could get to the canal and find a Belgian barge captain to hide me until he could hand me on down to Marseilles or some place beyond their world, beyond their horizon, I might get back.

Anyway, I left them and a day and a half after that my feet started to give out. I was wearing this guy's shoes which weren't my size. I saw a bicycle in front of a pub (it was the pub-keeper's bike, I found out many years later) and, imitating Tom Mix from a pre-war Hollywood picture, I raced across the road and leaped onto it, just about denaturing myself, and started to pedal furiously. I could hear a hue and cry behind me and just kept going. I got out of town into some woods, pulled the bicycle deep into them and buried it, covering it with leaves so the sun wouldn't reflect on it. Then I went a little deeper in the woods, found a little ditch, covered myself with leaves and waited. In due course, two Dutch policemen riding bicycles came down the road. They were obviously looking for me.

I told myself I should wait until nightfall and not walk in the daytime. After a few minutes, I said to myself, "I can't wait several hours. I'll wait an hour." So I waited fifty minutes and came out of the woods, without the bike, of course, and was just nicely out when this one copper came back on his bike and stopped me. He addressed me in Dutch, asked me where I was going.

I said, "Tilburg," which was a point on the map. Then he started to wave his sword, the only weapon carried by the local police at that time. He started to wave this thing around, so I said, "Slow down. I'm Royal Air Force. I'm trying to escape. If I get back I can tell my tale. I'm sure you don't like the Germans. I'll come back in an aircraft again and drop more bombs on them."

So he said, "Yes," and told me his name. "After the war you will write me?"

I replied, "Yes," and very solemnly we shook hands in the middle of this road and I started to walk away. I went in the wood and recovered the bicycle, while he headed back towards the town. Instinct should have told me to get the hell out of the way. But I didn't — I just went on down the road. Ten minutes later he was after me again, saying "Quislings have seen us. If I don't take you back, we'll both be shot." Well, he had this sword and didn't seem like a very nice guy and I wasn't in a position to argue. So we rode into town and went before the Burgermaster, who was a real son-of-a-bitch of a Quisling (obviously, if he hadn't been a Quisling, he wouldn't have been Burgermaster).

I said to this guy, who was smoking a cigar, "What's going to happen to me?"

He replied, "I must call the Luftwaffe to come and get you."

I said, "You don't really have to do that."

"Well, what option do I have?"

I said, "Why don't you just say I'm a Belgian and you've arrested me for stealing a bicycle."

"Oh, no. It's impossible."

At this point I didn't want to argue any more, so I made a break for it, got away and jumped into a bloody ditch. I was still picking stinging nettles out of my wrist when a cop took me back to his house. He was a newly-wed. He and his wife fed me supper, let me shave and the entire village turned out on the front lawn.

"When comes the invasion?"

What the hell could you tell these poor people as early as June, 1942? Then the Luftwaffe came for me and all these people gave me the great V-sign and that was that.

I had been shot down on the first bomber raid on Cologne and in the subsequent week there were several big raids on Bremen and Hamburg, and there were probably more RAF's walking around Holland than Dutchmen. A lot of us were collected in Amsterdam in a big cell block. Each of us was in solitary confinement. After about four days of solitary, the door burst open and in came four guys with big boots and leather jackets, just like in a spy movie. Their process of searching was much more diligent and thorough than that of the Luftwaffe. The Luftwaffe had found a map in my cap and that was about it. These types who came in insisted that they were *feldpolizei*, field security police, and weren't Gestapo, and had no connection with the SS. They started to rip. The escape kit carried by air crew on operations was the size of a cigarette package. Into that was packed all sorts of incriminating nonsense.

Anyway, as the *feldpolizei* ripped the collar of my red silk shirt, out came about 500 French francs. They ripped off a sleeve and out came a map. A big incriminating pile began to build up on the floor of the cell block and at that

point they ripped the sweatband on my pants and this hacksaw blade fell out. I can still hear it bouncing off the concrete floor, shattering the silence. It seemed a promise of eternity. At that point they marched me out to the hall. One guy had a Luger with the barrel coldly pressed against the back of my neck. It's a very persuasive feeling. There we stopped while another guy signed a receipt for the Luftwaffe for one enemy person, one body in good physical shape.

With the Luger still in my neck, I was marched to a Mercedes, in which we rode gangster-style across Amsterdam. Two of the thugs were in the front seat and two in the back, with me between them with my hands palming the low roof of the car and the Luger in my neck. Twice on the way across Amsterdam these chaps tried to mow down Jews with the car. It was about a month after the Jewish star had been introduced into Holland, and you'd see these elderly Jews with the yellow stars. The thugs did it not with the intention of scaring them but literally to try to mow them down with the front bumper.

We arrived at a great stone building which I subsequently learned was the Gestapo police headquarters. There were big vases of flowers in the entrance foyer, on the landing of the first floor, and on the landing of the second. I thought to myself, "Flowers, funerals, morgue. These sons-of-bitches are going to shoot me right where they don't have to haul the body." We went up five floors to a room where they stood me in a corner like a bad boy in a Sunday School class. Finally I was allowed to turn around and sit in a chair. There was an old, avuncular, friendly-looking Gestapo type sitting in a chair behind a big desk. A girl came in with a shoe box and I thought, "Oh, we're going to have a boxed lunch." Out came a pair of handcuffs, a pair of leg irons, and the biggest chain I've ever seen — to connect the handcuffs to the leg irons behind my back.

Now, the human body is symmetrical and if you sit thus equipped, the chain goes down between the cheeks of your rectum. Well, I'm seated in this chair with four Gestapo types, and one of the buggers was screaming at me in German for forty minutes and going through my head was the intelligence drill we used to get back in Britain. "If you're shot down and taken for interrogation, remain calm, retain your dignity, stare out of a window or at a distant wall." And I thought, "I wonder if that wingless son-of-a-bitch has ever sat with a chain up his ass?"

They wanted to know how I could prove that I was an airman. They were going to shoot me, and I said, "Well, I'm not in any position to argue with you."

They asked, "Who are your crew?"

I replied, "You tell me who my crew were and I'll tell you if you're right." And they did, which only confirmed that they knew very close to where I had come down.

In due course, I was sent to a prisoner-of-war camp. I was so terrified that somehow they would track down the family who had helped me that, for over twenty years, I just buried it in my mind. For all those years I wouldn't even try to recall where they had helped me or who they were. However, in the 1970's, I started to try to locate them through a colonel in the Royal Netherlands Airforce, who had done a great deal heading up the airforce efforts to locate aircraft and restore them, and to locate people who had been shot down there and to help locate people such as my benefactress and her family. I wrote to him and told him the story. He had one of his press officers in the Eindhoven area give it to the newspapers and the *Eindhoven Dagblatt* ran it. Within a week they had located the woman. Her son told them the story of my arrival at their house. This boy, who had been nine years of age at the time, was now, of course, about thirty-nine. The pub-keeper whose bicycle I had stolen recalled the incident and was so apologetic. If he had only known I was in the airforce and trying to escape, he would never have set up a hue and cry.

My wife and I went to Eindhoven and were reunited with my benefactress, the farmer's wife. Her husband had died and also her daughter, who had answered the door of the house. But her other daughters and her son and brother-in-law all came and we spent a day and a half there. With the reporters who had written the story, we walked to the Belgian border where she had led me at night and re-enacting the episode,   went to the loft where they had hidden me. In the course of the day and night we spent there, they presented us with an oil painting that they had commissioned of the farm house. My wife and I just broke up. My wife told me, "They're giving you this picture in gratitude to you for not turning them in to the Gestapo. You should have been so thankful to *them*."

Then my benefactress produced this compass. She had hidden it for thirty years and wouldn't part with it. It was a souvenir. What's more, she had kept my flying boots until the end of the war and then sold them with typical Dutch farm frugality, to a chap who worked with her husband at the local factory. More than that, she had taken my battledress jacket and pants, dyed them and made them into a coat that her daughter wore to school for three years of World War II, under the eyes of the Nazis!

32

Java

Paddy Leonard

from a taped interview

We capitulated in Java on March 8th, 1942. I was in Bandong at the airport, having supper one night, when a guy said to me, "Paddy, how would you like to take off?"

I said, "Sure."

He was in the airforce and he said, "We're going to get a bomber." There was an old bomber on the runway. He said, "We'll fix it up with bombay tanks." Which we did. Filled her with gasoline. There was a flight sergeant, whose name I won't mention, who said "If you attempt to take that aircraft, I'm going to tell the Japanese." Even so, we worked on it and one day we had it all ready to go. I met a Dutch pilot who said he would fly her out. There were two squadron leaders who said, "Yes, we'll take off." The wing was broken, so I said, "Well, I'll sit up there."

"This is going to be very cold, Paddy."

I said, "I don't mind, as long as I get the hell out of here."

When we went to get the aircraft, they had stuck knives

in the tires and rendered it unsafe to fly. Three days later, my friend, Dick Davis from Wales, said, "Paddy, we're going to make an attempt to escape." So I went with him, and Len Cooper, and Chuck Dunbar. We went down to the south coast and met some Australians who were trying to get away from the island. Len Cooper said, "Let's go towards Singapore."

I said, "No, because the Japanese are there. We'd better stay put in case someone comes to rescue us." But he took off anyway with Len, and they got captured.

Dick and I stayed on the island with the natives. We stayed for three months. They treated us tremendous. There was one little boy who had his hand cut across the palm. We put penicillin on it and tied it up and got it a little better and the natives couldn't do enough for us. They thought we were gods. I had pneumonia and they sent some children around to feed me lots of tea and sugar. They said, "You drink lots of that, tuan, it'll break your fever." Honest to God, it worked. It was better than taking quinine. Later two guys from inland called a doctor about this. He said, "Well, when did you have malaria last?"

I said, "Oh, three days ago."

He said, "I don't believe you. If you had, you wouldn't be here."

I said, "Well, I drank lots of sweet tea and sugar and it breaks the fever."

"Oh," he said, "I don't go for that. You're not going to get a pension." And that was it. That was someone who didn't have a clue how to treat people from the Far East who had run into problems. I had had dysentery, I had had beri-beri, pellagra. You name it, I've had it. Out in the Far East you get one little prick and it's infected right away. Pus keeps coming out and there's no cure. In prison camp you don't have any medication. Once, in hospital, I was next to a Dutchman and he had lice crawling all over him. So I said, "I want to get out of here" And he said something in Dutch which meant "ants". But it wasn't, it was lice. And I got out.

The toilet was across a creek, and the monsoons came and washed it away. The Indians used little bowls. They didn't use toilet paper. They cleaned their rectum with the water.

A Japanese died and they called us to collect firewood to cremate the guy. We got the fire going and I said to one of our fellows, "Who died?"

He said, "Oh, Donald Duck." That was the nickname we gave to the little bastard. I started to laugh and the Japanese sergeant came up and knocked the hell out of me, just knocked the shit out of me. He said, "Why are you laughing?"

I said, "Well, I come from Ireland. In Ireland we have wakes and weddings, we dance, we sing, we drink. What the hell, let's send the soul happy to God Almighty." He gave me a pack of cigarettes and knocked the hell out of every other guy that wouldn't laugh.

One day we were all called out in the rain. A man was missing and they searched everywhere and couldn't find him. He had fallen down the toilets and drowned. There was another guy who was hungry and stole a Japanese dog. He killed it and put it under his bedspace, which was a lot of boards. With the temperatures out there — you're looking at 130 degrees in the shade. They were going to have meat but, of course, it had gone rotten. They threw him in a cage and used sling shots on him. He eventually went out of his mind.

When I came to Sumatra, I was one of the few British persons who could speak fluent Malaysian, and I traded. Before that the Dutchmen did all the trading because they also spoke Malaysian. One day I went out with a big army overcoat on. I was so hot. The Japanese inspector said, "Why are you wearing that overcoat?"

I said, "I got malaria. I get cold." That night I came back minus the overcoat. I had sold it for ninety Dutch guilders. I did pretty well, but I took a risk.

Once an officer, Commander Bell, came to me and said, "Paddy, could you get some vegetables for this Australian guy?" I said, "Sure, I'll get some eggs and some lettuce." I went out that night, traded with the natives and I got the lettuce and eggs.

Of course, when I went out through the wire, it was difficult getting back. One night I went out and the Japanese came right after me. I got back before them and when they returned they were holding a ground-sheet, demanding to know who had been trying to sell it. I had dropped it in the jungle. Pity. I could have got fifteen guilders for it.

Anyway, when I got the eggs and lettuce for this Australian guy, he said, "I'm not a rabbit. I don't eat that stuff." Well, he died a week later with beri-beri. His stomach got so high, they cut it open and the water flew out just like somebody turned the faucet on. The guy died. I did my best.

When we were finally liberated, I had pneumonia and pleurisy and was very, very sick. The British troops came marching through. Tears rolled down my cheeks. Later I was in the British General Hospital in Singapore for six weeks.

But I never got my pension.

33

Train Jumping

Rod McKenzie

from a taped interview

We were working in the bush on the Polish border. Some fellows had escaped from the place and the Germans decided there would be no more. So they reinforced the windows, which had been barred in the first place.

We had occasion to go out and fight a forest fire. We came home with a couple of spare axes and put them to use to remove the mortar from the windows.

Three of us went the same night. I was on the loose for eight days. A second was out for eight weeks, while it was nine months before they caught up with the third one. They were with the Polish partisans.

When you're out you feel the whole world against you. You're in a country with a lot of wild pigs and you hear them going through the brush at night. Any noise, a dog barking six miles away, could be heard in the open country; you figured he was right behind you.

I got through that border area; it was no problem, and I registered in a little village. They had to account for everybody that was in the village. They accepted my Canadian Army paper because it was an official document! I don't think it was stamped or anything. I still have it.

I kept wandering away and not really knowing where I was going. I thought I was heading towards Warsaw. I heard a train going by one day and I thought I'd jump it; it's a lot faster than hiking. I got in position to run and catch it. Suddenly all I could see along that open door on the train was jack boots hanging out. Of all things it was a German troop train that I was going to jump! That changed my mind.

So I stayed in hiding. I finally got a train, one of those gondola cars, the coal car. I got into one of them and I got up to Kiel.

34
Reunion In Italy

Fred Milner

After two years of desert fighting, from June, 1940, to June, 1942, and frequent dive-bombing by Stukas, I began my prisoner-of-war life with an air bombardment from our own aircraft.

This was at El Adem airfield where our German captors had marshalled us. Airforce and army technological personnel were being identified and flown directly to Germany. To avoid such a trip, I masqueraded as a Cameron Highlander. I buried my dog-tag and paybook in the sand nearby, retrieving them when the German guards had passed.

Eventually, we were force-marched northwards (temperature — 116 degrees F) to the outskirts of Tobruk where we were handed over to the Italians. We were then trucked westwards and counted by the hundreds into the hell-hole of the Derna graveyard where we competed with the flies for space, and fought for breath in the ovenlike temperature.

Those of us with dysentery spent sleepless nights by

the latrine pits (no wooden seats) which were soon filled to overflowing. Space being at a premium meant some luckless souls had no choice but to share space at the 'ringside' with the infected. For two whole weeks no one enjoyed the luxury of being able to stretch out full length on the ground at night. We slept on our backs, with knees bent and pointed to the sky.

Having successfully run the gauntlet of British submarines and surface craft by dashing under escort across the Mediterranean via the coast of Greece, we disembarked at Taranto in southern Italy. We arrived exhausted and undernourished, suffering from desert sores, lice and beri beri. After a train journey to Brindisi, we were marched like the captives of Rome in ancient times in triumph through the streets. Our destination was a 'de-bugging' centre on the edge of town. Two of my companions were spat upon by a group of people as we passed. The same people would probably have been surprised and shocked to discover that they were spitting on German captives and not prisoners of the glorious Fascist state as they were led by propaganda to believe. By now, in the desert war, the Germans allowed few Italian troops to fight in the front line, but they were pretty much in evidence doing echelon work carrying supplies.

Our first Italian prisoner-of-war camp was a tent encampment at Altamura some miles inland west of Bari. This place was a disaster. Weeks passed and no food parcels got through despite the fact that the Allies had not yet even invaded Sicily.

It was rumoured that the Italians were starving, consequently those food parcels which survived Allied bombing were being pilfered. The only medical supply in the camp was aspirin. Our plight grew worse as our meagre rations (two hundred grams of bread, i.e. 6 oz., and one pint of 'skilly' or watered macaroni, daily) took a toll on our health and morale.

Food and lice were our greatest concerns. A brief visit

from an emissary of the Pope resulted in a gift of a piano accordion and a few pious words. We desperately sought ways to add variety to our diet by collecting thyme which we discovered growing in the camp. Our daily bread loaf was cut in half, the soft insides removed and mixed with thyme and water. When replaced and roasted, it weighed heavy and fulfilled a need. My stomach has never been the same since.

Finally, the International Red Cross arrived and condemned the camp as being below the standards required by the Geneva Convention.

We were then transported northwards by rail in cattle cars to PG 73, situated between Modena and Florence. Another tent lager greeted us, but two hut compounds were being built close by. It was a race against the onset of winter and we made it in time to spend our first Christmas, for many of us, since 1939, in permanent accommodation. Furthermore, food parcels, one between six (one between two for Christmas) had arrived to great rejoicing. Nevertheless, throughout the whole of our captivity we only once had the luxury of a whole parcel each.

Throughout our stay in PG 73, we never received any improvement in our Italian rations. At best, the 'skilly' would be served a little thicker, but never at any time contained even one potato. Our food parcels, although irregular in supply, and divided into miniscule amounts, saved us from complete starvation.

The news of the Italian capitulation reached us one evening in September, 1943. The Italian Kommandant talked us into remaining in the camp that evening because, he said, there were 'scattered remnants of fascist troops roaming the countryside, and, in any case, a landing of Allied troops in northern Italy is imminent.'

At dawn, a German panzer regiment surrounded the camp and disarmed the Italian guards. We were 'in the bag' again, cursing ourselves for having listened to that camp Kommandant.

Thereafter, it was a case of awaiting rail transportation to Germany. In the few weeks which followed, our rations improved; more parcels arrived (one between three) from a nearby officers' camp. Nevertheless, despite the prospect of better rations in German camps, the presence of German guards seemed to motivate everyone's desire to escape. Thus, escape activity filled our waking hours — tunnels were built, which were either discovered or collapsed, fortunately without loss of life. Three guys, according to plan, went out with the garbage. Only one was returned, and he was put on display for hours between the two wire fences which surrounded the camp, then put in solitary.

There were roughly one thousand prisoners in each compound. As one emptied its occupants enroute for Germany, we would sneak into it under the cover of the shadows created by the huts. Guards along this section of the fence had been withdrawn and we spent many hours tossing stones at the lights when the guards in the watch towers were preoccupied. We drew lots one night; two of us got through the fence, then there was a yell, and a searchlight followed by bullets crashed through the stillness of the Italian evening.

Two days later we were marched along the country roads to the railway station. The last thing I snatched from the door before leaving was a notice which we used as a target when playing darts. Enroute to the station a small group of prisoners, at a prearranged signal, made a run for it through the grape vines, but the majority was either recaptured, or cut down by the German guards who chose their targets at leisure, firing from one knee at their retreating legs. At the sight of their dash for freedom we cheered loudly as if at a football match.

We were counted, forty at a time, into the cattle cars. Two crates of loaves and carrots were tossed inside and the doors slammed shut.

My bid for freedom came during the journey. Once

again we had to endure the chilling experience of sweating it out in an air raid knowing that the bomb aimer above was one of our boys. I can testify to the resulting devastation but miraculously our train wasn't hit. In the light of the explosions and flares, I detected the screws which held in place the ventilator at floor level. After a hurried consultation with my neighbours, a spoon with a flattened handle and a small army jackknife with a screwdriver butt at one end were produced. Only one companion, Joe, volunteered to join me in my labours. The others were of the opinion that German camps would be better, and that the war would end in a year or so anyway.

The train was soon on the move again and we set to work on the ventilator. Suddenly we stopped and guards came down the track thumping the sides of our cars with their rifles and machine guns, shining their torches and noisily discussing the air raid. Joe and I stared at one another. The sweat on our faces illuminated briefly as they shone their torch through the grills of the ventilator. We held our breath and they passed on.

A few miles down the track, Joe removed the ventilator and as I went through the hole head first, he held my ankles while I explored the possibilities of handholds and footholds outside. The train lurched from side to side, gathering speed on the level and sloping gradients. We were approaching the Alps and the Brenner Pass. As we came to a bend I detected a passenger car filled with guards at the end of the train. By now it was a moonlit night, though not a full moon. I signalled with my foot to be hauled back into the car. We agreed that the safest way to avoid falling beneath the wheels was to climb out, pause momentarily on the buffers, and then jump, thus reducing the risk of losing one's balance. It was decided that at the next slow section of line, I would go first and wait thirty minutes after I landed for Joe to join me.

I landed with a thump, wrenching my shoulder. The cars looming above me rattled past, guards and all, oblivous of me lying at the bottom of the embankment. Fifty yards along the track there began a concrete buttress and wall of a bridge. I shuddered for Joe, and then for myself as I realized what might happen to him and what could have happened to me had I delayed my jump long enough to hit the wall of the bridge.

I waited for what seemed a lifetime. Finding a vineyard, I ran amok, pressing the grapes greedily into my mouth with their juices making rivulets down my chin. I was free! God, how my heart sang!

A light beam, of what later proved to be a searchlight, manned by German guards at an Italian hydro-power station, flitted briefly among the leaves. I later determined that I was southwest of Bolzano, not far south of the Brenner Pass.

I had many adventures before climbing two mountain ranges north of pass Stelvio into Switzerland, arriving at a small village called Santa Maria where I was interned from November, 1943, to October, 1944. My buddy and I had the good fortune to be aided by a girl, Rosina, who doggedly guided us over a mountain range, escorting us carefully past snow-covered crevices to reach the safety of a guide's home in the valley beyond. When my buddy, suffering from mountain sickness, flagged, she insisted on carrying his small pack containing our few belongings despite my protestations that I could carry the load myself. We both still felt the effects of our prison deprivation, yet we climbed upwards, refusing to accept defeat in the eyes of a 'woman mountaineer'.

For many years after the war, I promised myself that one day I would return to Italy to thank Rosina. I made a half-hearted attempt in 1955 when, having purchased my first little British car, my wife and I drove into Italy. We toured the Italian roads, studying the map intently. I became quite enthusiastic and nostalgic as we debated how we could reach her home, the mountain village of Cognolo, situated on the Italian-Swiss border north of pass Stelvio.

It had been different in 1943, I thought, for in those days when a mountain blocked our path we climbed it. But now, in 1955, somewhat softened by married life in 'civvy street' and restricted to road travel, mountains appeared as unsurmountable barriers. Add to that discouragement, my wife's repeated reminder of the promise I had made to two English schoolteachers, to transport them back to England from Lausanne, Switzerland, and I was finally influenced to abandon my quest.

Throughout the next few years my conscience periodically bothered me. A familiar scene would flash through my mind. It would be that of a young woman sitting patiently and disconsolately on a boulder in front of a mountain guide's small house, as my buddy and I bargained with his Rolex watch for a safe conduct over the remaining mountain range into Switzerland.

Our subsequent crossing of the final range of mountains, and the dramatic moment when we crossed the border negotiating barbed wire, and evading Swiss military ski patrols came back to me vividly one day last summer as I was cleaning out some old correspondence. I came across two letters written in Italian, both from Rosina, and dated 1945 and 1946. I remembered obtaining a rough verbal translation from an Italian barber, shortly after arriving in Canada, the gist of which was that I had promised Rosina to return to Italy after the war if I survived. As I gazed at the two letters, my feeling of guilt returned. I pondered for a while; then I suddenly made up my mind. I couldn't go on feeling guilty forever. I would try to locate Rosina and her sister, visit them in Italy, and try to express my heartfelt gratitude for their brave assistance. If I failed after a determined attempt, maybe my conscience would be stilled forever.

Judy, my understanding wife, agreed with my plans and suggested I go alone. If she suspected romance was involved, even at my age, she certainly didn't betray any such notion.

The Italian consular official in Hamilton sounded as though a request to re-unite people after thirty-seven years of separation was an everyday occurrence. "I will ring you back," the voice said in response to my request for the whereabouts of Rosina Caserotti, one-time resident of Cogolo.

One hour later the phone rang. "There are four people (all males) answering to the name of Caserotti living in Cogolo," the voice said. "Their names are Attilio, Dino, Ignio, and Pio."

"How would you know so quickly?" I asked.

"By consulting the phone book," the voice answered. It was so simple that I felt rather foolish after anticipating a prolonged search. But there were no phones in Cogolo in 1943, I thought defensively. Times change, I reminded myself with some alarm, and perhaps Rosina is dead! The voice then supplied me with the address of an interpreter, Mrs. De Vincent, who would translate my letters into good written English if required.

After reading the English translation obtained later from Mrs. De Vincent, I felt even more guilty, for in one passage Rosina reminded me of my promise to return. I quickly wrote a letter to the Caserottis of Cogolo, asking for the address of Rosina which Mrs. De Vincent translated into Italian before mailing it to Italy.

My flight to England was booked and I bought a Eurorail ticket, for I now planned to travel initially to England and then to Denmark and Switzerland, looking up old friends enroute. Thus, I reasoned, by the time I reached Denmark or Switzerland, my wife would be able to phone or mail Rosina's new address.

I was in Denmark ten days later when I received a phone call from Judy, indicating that Rosina's letter (in Italian) gave her new address as Brescia, about one hour by train east of Milan. Judy was obtaining a translation from Mrs. De Vincent and would mail it to my address in Switzerland, but expressed fears about its arrival because of a mail strike in Ontario.

After waiting three days in Switzerland without receiving any news, I decided to catch the train to Milan, trusting that the address Judy had given me over the phone was all I needed anyway. I felt more anxious about kidnappings, ransom money, and bombed railway stations than I did about the accuracy of Judy's interpretation of Rosina's address. Before leaving Switzerland, my Swiss friend, who spoke some Italian, volunteered to communicate with Rosina if I was able to phone her. A man's voice answered to the number I eventually dialled and I handed the phone to my friend. They spoke briefly and when my friend finally hung up she told me I had the correct address and I was to hire a cab at the railway station in Brescia.

As my train sped towards Milan, I leaned back thoughtfully in my seat. Rosina would not be at the station, I thought. Did this mean I would still be welcome after all these years? I was wearing a blazer with the Canadian National Prisoner-of-War emblem sewn on the breast pocket. Maybe that would help recognition? But how would her husband welcome me? I was now convinced that the man who answered the phone was her husband. Perhaps my prisoner-of-war badge would symbolize my honourable intentions? Italian husbands I knew had a reputation for being jealous. Would this one be philosophical about such a reunion? After all, Judy, my wife, was philosophical, although she could really be possessive when aroused. I dismissed my thoughts and prepared myself for the Italian immigration and custom officers.

Milan station looked rather seedy after the neat, clean Swiss railway stations, but it was busy and full of anxious-looking passengers, hurrying to catch their respective train connections. I found my train, and was soon on the last leg of my journey to Brescia. My compartment was crowded. A mother and her bambino kept us all entertained. A priest sitting on my left competed with me in being the quickest to pick up the baby's toys which included a pacifier and an empty chocolate wrapper. I was grateful for the diversion, because now that I was nearing Brescia I became quietly excited. It was the priest who murmured "Brescia", alerting me instantly when the train pulled into the station. We both clambered out and, in response to my inquiry, pointed to the place where I could hire a taxi.

I was ready for this moment with the taxi driver. Silently I handed him a card showing Rosina's address, then said one word (remembered from World War II) "Avanti!" and 'avanti' we did! We sped through the streets and I anxiously watched the taxi meter, partially hidden by the rear of the front seat. "Quanto lira?" I asked. I understood his reply to mean two thousand and something — and, after handing him three thousand (about ten dollars), I received 500 lire change. Simple! I thought, there is absolutely no truth at all in the rumour about being ripped off in Italy.

I stepped out of the cab and found myself face to face with two ladies and a third, who looked like a ~~daugher~~. One of the ladies looked familiar and we stared at each other for a few seconds before recognition dawned. Rosina and I shook hands and kissed on each cheek. Her sister Ada, and daughter, Dominique, stood smiling from ear to ear; as I turned to them they gave me a similar welcome. It was just like a family reunion! After the introductions were over, I quickly became conscious of my surroundings. A sidewalk cafe was behind us, which was part of a huge apartment complex. Rosina led me across the sidewalk into the apartment building to meet her husband, Alfonso.

Alfonso Nota proved to be a genial good-natured concierge, but his job by contrast would be the envy of any building superintendent in Canada. He seemed to spend the day either supervising a huge console of white buttons giving him telephone communication to those apartment dwellers who called, or giving orders to his innumerable helpers. He was a supervisor in the real sense, and seemed to be respected by those who dwelt there, including one American resident who claimed to be a retired vice-

president of the American Standard Oil Company. I was
relieved to find that I did not have a jealous Italian husband on my hands.

During the first few hours, we talked endlessly, aided
by one of the apartment dwellers, an English schoolteacher
married to an Italian, who acted as our interpreter. Questions had to be answered. Why hadn't I written? Had I been
well treated in Switzerland? Did my health improve? Was
I married? Etc.

I explained that in 1943 we were warned in
Switzerland not to communicate by letter, or indeed any
way, with the people in Italy who helped us, in case of
German retribution. And during the years immediately after
the war my health had deteriorated and, consequently, I
didn't want to be reminded of my wartime experiences.
I pointed out in my own defence, as Rosina looked momentarily resentful, that I had attempted once to reach Cogolo,
her village, in 1955, in my little British car, for by then I
had regained my physical and mental health.

Rosina told me that the day after Vincent and I left
Cogolo in October, 1943, the Germans surrounded the
village and questioned all the inhabitants. I shuddered, for
I remembered vividly what they did in those days with the
occupants of houses who harboured escaped prisoners-of-
war. Only those involved in this game of 'hide and seek',
as we were, knew how brave Rosina and her sister, Ada,
had been.

Ada interrupted my thoughts to remind me of the day
my buddy and I staggered in on the two girls who were
tending their father's cattle on the higher Alpine pastures.
We looked exhausted, she said, and laughingly reminded
me of how suspicious I was of the minestra (milk and
macaroni) she gave us and how reluctant I was, unlike my
friend, who was married, to strip off all my soaking wet
clothes in front of a huge fire. Rosina proudly produced
a certificate signed by Field-Marshal Alexander, presented
to her father, Christofer Caserotti, for helping members of

the Allied forces to avoid capture or re-capture.

The next day, a nephew was introduced to me who spoke German and, through him, I was able to communicate. Alfonso and Rosina owned a small house near Lake Garda, a tourist resort a few miles north of Brescia. Perhaps I would like to see it? Ada, who, I learned, worked in the administrative offices of Trentino University, was on holiday and wanted to visit Lake Garda, too, for her daughter and son-in-law managed a cafe there. Thus, after lunch was over, Ada, Rosina, and I piled into a little Fiat with Ada driving. Alfonso generously trusted his wife to my care, I thought, for he remained behind to look after his apartments.

As we drove along, Ada's high spirits were infectious. She led us all into singing the old wartime songs such as "Lili Marlene' and 'The White Cliffs of Dover' and, flushed with wine, we responded with gusto. Nevertheless, my Canadian driving experience, with its cautious habits, soon led me to scrutinize Ada's performance at the wheel as she darted in and out of the city traffic. Once on the highway, I felt reassured as to her ability, and continued singing with enjoyment. We were re-living those momentous days of October, 1943. This was an emotional incident during my visit which amply repaid all my efforts to return.

We stayed a few hours beside Lake Garda, enjoying the scenic beauty and the amenities the resort provided. It was late September and most visitors had departed. I took several photographs of my companions which I treasure among the souvenirs of my visit. Ada eventually returned to Trentino University and Rosina and I went back to Brescia by bus.

When it came time for me to return to Switzerland, where I had left the bulk of my luggage with friends, Rosina wouldn't hear of my spending money on a taxi to reach Brescia railway station. We travelled by bus and periodically she spoke animatedly with fellow passengers she recognized. Only once, to save me embarrassment, I suspect, did I become the subject of their conversation. Not understanding Italian, I could only smile, but I felt at ease and very happy.

On the station platform, we learned that my train would be twenty-five minutes late but Rosina insisted on remaining until it arrived. I grew anxious because it was now raining and she wore only a thin dress. Just like the war years, I thought, she would stay by my side until she was satisfied that I was safely on my way.

The rain had stopped when the train arrived and her last word to me before we kissed and said goodbye, was a question, "Contente?" she asked.

And I replied, "Si Si, Rosina."

She stood smiling on the platform waving goodbye and, after thirty-seven years, I was indeed content.

35

Heroine Of The Resistance

R. L. Masters
from a taped interview

This is the story of a woman who in the 1914-1918 war billeted Canadian soldiers in her little farm house near the front lines. She never abandoned the house regardless of where the fighting was and during that time she met many Canadian soldiers. After that war, during which she lost her husband, she raised her children, always hoping that one day some of her Canadian soldiers would come and visit in peace time. Unfortunately most of those soldiers when they went home married and raised families, struggling through the Depression and leaving little hope that they would return.

On Midsummer Night 1943 I arrived in Belgium on an unscheduled flight, having just been through to the Ruhr valley and unable to return to our base because our aircraft had been damaged to the point where it refused to fly much further. It was just before daybreak on June 22nd when I found myself hiding out in a wooded area on the edges of a little lake called Silvermeer. I had no idea what country I was in. I was fortunate that it turned out to be Belgium. It was right at the intersection of the German, Belgian and Dutch borders so I could have been in any of the three countries.

After hiding out for the daylight hours when obviously the bush-beating by the Germans would have detected me, I felt it would be safe to emerge and try to make contact with somebody. Just as it was getting towards dusk I came out of my hiding-place and found myself on a country lane a couple of hundred yards from where I had been. After walking a few minutes I came upon a village inn. There was possibly a dozen people in the inn, workers who had finished for the day. Among them was a man who headed a small group of Resistance workers who had been looking for members of our crew, trying to find them before the Germans did. I was the only one who had evaded capture at this point. It took a few minutes for these people to settle back after my arrival because I didn't appreciate the fact that when a large airplane crashes in the neighbourhood that it's bound to arouse a lot of interest. They knew instantly who I was, even though I cut the badges off my uniform.

The greeting I received in that pub was one to be remembered, with the women kissing me on both cheeks and men shaking my hand right hand, left hand, it didn't matter to them; until finally one chap who spoke very good English, a Mr. Fruithov, came up and said, "This is a very dangerous situation that we have here. Let's get you out."

So this was my introduction to the Resistance movement. I was taken out to the back and hidden in the garden between rows of peas where the height of the vegetation was sufficient to obscure me from the road. After a few minutes Mr. Fruitov showed up with a bicycle. I got on it with him, and in a most uncomfortable manner managed to leave the area just as it was getting dark, to spend the night hiding, this time with friends and not on my own.

It was to be only a matter of two or three weeks when

Civilians in occupied Europe watch grounded aircraft.

I would be living with a family in Brussels by the name of Bulpa. This was the Madame Bulpa who had never seen the return of her Canadian soldiers from the First World War. I would loved to have said I will come back and visit you after this whole thing is over, but I was reluctant to commit myself to something that I had no idea whether I could accomplish, and so the most I could say was that I hoped I would be able to come back during less dangerous times when we could walk the streets and speak regardless of what language it was and enjoy being free of the oppressive atmosphere that was to prevail throughout the fabric of everyday life.

During the more than six months that I was in the Resistance movement I met many people and it always seemed to me that Madame Bulpa most represented the spirit of these people at that time. So when I was able to return one spring, seventeen years later, to a cottage on the outskirts of Brussels, to visit the Bulpa family and many other friends it seemed that I had come back to fullfil an old obligation on behalf of the soldiers who couldn't return after the First World War.

I was greeted when I arrived by a circle of people waiting at the head of the drive as I drove up in a little rented car. As I got out of the car it was almost a re-enactment of the first time that I had walked into the village inn in Mol in 1943. We had a glorious re-union, with a tremendous buffet that was the epitome of luxury as if we were trying to show ourselves the other side of the hard-times coin we lived through during the Occupation.

The centrepiece of this for me was the old woman who had waited so many years to see one of her boys come back to visit. During the course of the evening many toasts were celebrated. It seemed that every time there was space in a conversation, and every time a glass was raised Madame Bulpa struggled to her feet to partake, sometimes laughing through tears, at other times just laughing.

I think the part that really drove home how much this visit meant to these people was — when we returned home we heard in a letter from the family that the old lady had died that following July. Instead of feeling sad — because it comes to us all — I was grateful that I had been able to make the visit in time.

36

The British Free Corps

(The following "message" was delivered to all POW camps containing British servicemen. Almost without exception the leaflets, provided by The British Free Corps, were treated with amusement or immediately burned in front of the German guards. The so-called Free Corps was an attempt by the German government to enlist British POWs as a unit to fight with the Germans on the Russian Front.)

As a result of repeated applications from British subjects from all parts of the world wishing to take part in the common European struggle against Bolshevism, authorisation has recently been given for the creation of a British volunteer unit.

The British Free Corps publishes herewith the following short statement of the aims and principles of the unit.

1) The British Free Corps is a thoroughly British volunteer unit, conceived and created by British subjects from all parts of the Empire who have taken up arms and pledged their lives in the common European struggle against Soviet Russia.

2) The British Free Corps condemns the war with Germany and the sacrifice of British blood in the interests of Jewry and International Finance, and regards this conflict as a fundamental betrayal of the British People and British Imperial interests.

3) The British Free Corps desires the establishment of peace in Europe, the development of close friendly relations between England and Germany, and the encouragement of mutual understanding and collaboration between the two great Germanic peoples.

4) The British Free Corps will neither make war against Britain or the British Crown, or support any action or policy detrimental to the interests of the British People.

Published by the British Free Corps

37

Albert

Donald G. Campbell
from a taped interview

I was a Warrant Officer in 403 Squardron and was shot down on June 2, 1942 over the English Channel. After spending one year in Stalag 8B, I was transferred, with eleven other Warrant Officers, to Milag and Marlag O. The Germans, being sticklers for regulations, thought we should have officers' treatment.

Marlag O was a very good camp with 400 men. There was a compound nearby for merchant seamen. Once a week we were taken about a quarter of a mile away to the showers.

Always on our minds were thoughts of ways to escape. It would be easy for a prisoner to remain in the shower while all the others returned to the camp and to make his escape after nightfall, as the showers weren't guarded. However, the prisoners were counted as they came back into the camp marching three abreast. Then someone came up with the idea of making a dummy. Each man would carry a small piece of it to the shower where it would be assembled and its arms would be fixed to the arms of two prisoners. We had some really talented fellows in our camp and when we got him all together from bits and pieces of stuff we had scrounged, he was quite a handsome fellow. He became known as "Albert".

With Albert's help, several men were able to get out of the camp. He would be taken out on parade until the Escape Committee felt that the escapee had had plenty of time. The Germans couldn't understand how they were getting out. They searched for tunnels and holes in the wire.

One day we were coming back from the showers with Albert marching along between his two buddies. He looked like a real sea-dog, in his naval cap and great-coat. A cigarette was stuck between his teeth. As we approached the gate there must have been twenty or twenty-five guards waiting for us. Even in the distance we knew that we had been found out. As the first three men entered the gate they were examined very carefully. When the two supporting Albert arrived, he was easily spotted. The anger of those German guards knew no bounds. Poor Albert was torn limb from limb, kicked and stamped upon and the two men who walked with him got two months of solitary confinement.

(Editor's note: Albert the dummy was the subject of a West End play by British playwright Guy Morgan.)

38

Envoi

Hugh Mooney

Si je meure demain trop tot
J'espere qu'il existe un ami
Qui va verser une larme ou deux
Pour moi;
Et si je meure sans priere,
Laisse-moi coucher tout seul
Parmi les cendres;
Et toi,
Qui est ami, oublies tes prieres,
Je ne les voudrais pas,
Parce que je vais d'ou je vins,
En l'oubli.